The Politics
of Education
in the States

The Bobbs-Merrill Policy Analysis Series

The Politics
of Education
in the States

Harmon Zeigler
and
Karl F. Johnson

THE BOBBS-MERRILL COMPANY, INC.
Indianapolis • New York

James A. Robinson
Macalester College
CONSULTING EDITOR IN POLITICAL SCIENCE

Thomas R. Dye
Florida State University
GENERAL EDITOR, *The Bobbs-Merrill Policy Analysis Series*

Foreword

The aim of the Policy Analysis Series is the systematic explanation of the content of public policy. The focus of the Series is on public policy choices of national, state, and local governments, and the forces that operate to shape policy decisions.

Books in the Policy Analysis Series are not concerned with what policies governments *ought* to pursue, but rather with *why* governments pursue the policies that they do. Public policies are not debated or argued in these volumes, rather they are assembled, described, and explained in a systematic fashion.

Each volume deals with an important area of public policy— education, taxing and spending, economic opportunity, agriculture, urban problems, military affairs. Each volume treats public policy as an output of political systems and endeavors to explain policy outputs with reference to historical, environmental, political, and cultural forces that generate demands upon political systems. Each volume attempts to employ systematic comparative analysis in the explanation of public policy. This involves the comparison of policies past and present; the comparison of policies generated by national, state, and local political systems; and the comparison of the effects of political, environmental, and cultural forces in the shaping of public policy. Each volume strives for improved theoretical statements about public policy determination.

Thomas R. Dye

Preface

The Politics of Education in the States presents a general theory of educational policy making in the American states that is systematic, comprehensive, and well researched. The authors disclaim any attempt to develop a general theory of resource allocation in political systems, but that is precisely what they have done. They have drawn upon a wide range of ideas, concepts, and method in political science —from systems theory and economic analysis, group theory, legislative process research, and attitudinal and behavioral studies—to develop a comprehensive picture of educational policy making.

Employing a general systems framework, Professors Zeigler and Johnson approach educational policy making by examining the complex interplay between environmental forces, the characteristics of political systems, the personal characteristics, attitudes, and behaviors of policy makers, the activities of interest groups, and educational policy outcomes. The authors move easily from "macro" analysis of the impact of economic resources, taxes and revenues, region, party competition, and political participation on educational outputs of the states to "micro" analysis of the policy impact of the "progressivism-liberalism" of individual legislators, their attitudes toward education, their relationships with education lobbyists, their age and social background, and their relationship with their constituents. More importantly, the authors have also undertaken to examine the linkages between these two levels of analysis: the interconnections between aggregate, economic, social, and political characteristics of states and the beliefs, attitudes, and behaviors of state legislators toward education. Statistical data from all fifty states are employed in their aggregate analysis of the educational outputs of whole political systems, and interview data from state legislators from Oregon, Massachusetts, North Carolina, and Utah are employed in their close-up examination of what happens *within* political systems.

The Politics of Education in the States presents a wide variety of original research findings. A sampling of these would include the following: educational expenditures are more closely related to economic resources than to any political or social variable; when economic resources are controlled, educational innovations are closely related to Democratic voting and party competition; legislative leaders are found to be more conservative on the question of increased taxes for education than rank-and-file legislators; wealthy, college educated legislators were found to be more favorable toward education than middle income, non-college educated legislators; the attitudes of legislators toward education corresponded to the states ranking in educational achievement, but legislators' general attitudes toward education were not very closely related to voting on specific educational bills.

Throughout the volume, Professors Zeigler and Johnson review and discuss a great deal of previous research and writing on education and public policy generally. They provide an excellent bibliography of materials on these topics, a list of data sources, and national means and specific scores for their sample states on many selected variables.

Thomas R. Dye

Acknowledgments

The authors wish to acknowledge the support of the Center for the Advanced Study of Educational Administration. The CASEA is a national research and development center which was established under the Cooperative Research Program of the U.S. Office of Education. The research reported in this study was conducted as part of the research and development program of the Center. The opinions expressed in this book do not necessarily reflect the position or policy of the U.S. Office of Education and no official endorsement by the Office of Education should be inferred.

Contents

Tables

Figures

The Politics
of Education
in the States

chapter 1

Introduction: Educational Policy Making and Political Theory

The research to be described in these pages attempts to provide answers to two questions, namely, How are educational resources allocated in the fifty American states? and How do state legislators approach the budgeting and financing of education? While not attempting to propose a grand theory of resource allocation, we do seek in this work to establish some relationships conducive to theory building.[1]

The need for more coherent theory regarding the distribution of resources in the states is genuine. Every year state legislators allocate more than $40 billion for various services touching every aspect of our lives; of this amount, over one-third is delegated to the support of education.[2] Thomas H. Eliot, president of Washington University in St. Louis, suggests that research is needed at the state level on

(a) the organization and financial administration of the state's educational activities; and (b) the pressures on the legislatures and

---

[1] See Robert Dubin, *Theory Building* (New York: The Free Press, 1969), pp. 5–11, and 87–95 for a discussion of the interrelationships between data, hypothesis testing, and theory building.

[2] Council of State Governments, *The Book of the States: 1964–65* (Chicago: Council of State Governments, 1964), p. 306.

the response to those pressures. The view . . . is that state action, especially in the legislatures, is now significant and will soon have a crucial impact on educational development, and that useful findings can result from a comparative study of state influence, management or control.[3]

Eliot's statement calls for—and the vast expenditures on education warrant—an analysis of the interactions between a state's environment, and its educational policies. In addition, we should also examine the pressures on state legislators and their attitudes.

Eliot's call for greater study of "the organization and financial administration of the state's educational activities" has been answered by only a few political scientists investigating general expenditure trends among the states.[4] Moreover, only recently has educational policy making at the city level been examined by any political scientists.[5] Researchers have carried out specialized studies concerning school district expenditures, school elections, and educational finances in particular states, but seldom have they focused on the impact of state legislatures on educational outcomes.[6] Studies of state legislators'

[3] Thomas H. Eliot, "Toward an Understanding of Public School Politics," *American Political Science Review* 52 (December 1959): 1051.

[4] See Thomas R. Dye, *Politics, Economics, and the Public: Policy Outcomes in the American States* (Chicago: Rand McNally, 1966); Ira Sharkansky, *Spending in the American States* (Chicago: Rand McNally, 1968); Richard I. Hofferbert, "The Relation Between Public Policy and Some Structural and Environmental Variables in the American States," *American Political Science Review* 60 (March 1966): 73–82; Richard I. Hofferbert, "Ecological Development and Policy Change in the American States," *Midwest Journal of Political Science* 10 (November 1966): 464–83; and Richard E. Dawson and James A. Robinson, "Interplay Competition, Economic Variables, and Welfare Politics in the American States," *Journal of Politics* 25 (May 1963): 265–89.

[5] See Thomas R. Dye, "Governmental Structure, Urban Environment, and Educational Policy," *Midwest Journal of Political Science* 11 (February 1967): 353–80; and H. Thomas James, James A. Kelly, and Walter I. Garms, *Determinants of Educational Expenditures in Large Cities in the United States* (East Lansing, Mich.: Cooperative Research Projects, Michigan State University, 1966), Project No. 2389.

[6] For example, see H. Thomas James, J. Alan Thomas, and Harold J. Dyck, *Wealth, Expenditure, and Decision-Making for Education* (Stanford, Calif.: Stanford University School of Education, 1963), Cooperative Research Project 1241; and George M. Beal, Virgil Lagomarcino, and John J. Hartman, *Iowa School Bond Issues: Summary Report* (Ames, Iowa: Iowa State University,

influence on educational outcomes are especially rare.[7] Our own research was specifically designed to bridge this gap. We seek in this study to link (1) the socioeconomic characteristics of the states with the individual characteristics of the state legislators, (2) the characteristics of those legislators with the various educational policy outcomes, and (3) the structural features of the legislatures with the legislators.

Hence, the problem that we have undertaken to study has two aspects: (1) no theory yet exists that adequately explains why state resources are allocated for education as they are, and (2) the explanations thus far proffered regarding educational allocations deliberately subordinate the importance of political factors. We propose in this study to add to the foundations for an adequate theory and to demonstrate that political variables are useful in explaining educational allocations.

To aid us in this pursuit we have constructed a model based on David Easton's input-output model (see Figure 1–1, p. 9).[8] We shall consider this model in two steps, first introducing the concepts from the Easton framework and then expanding them and relating them explicitly to what we are attempting to accomplish.

The Systems Model: A Theoretical Framework

State legislatures operate in an environment shared by other political systems.[9] This observation suggests that we must explore the "inputs"

Department of Sociology and Anthropology, 1966), Rural Sociology Report No. 61.

[7] Nicholas A. Masters, Robert H. Salisbury, and Thomas H. Eliot, *State Politics and the Public Schools* (New York: Alfred A. Knopf, 1964). For the only study available specifically on legislators' attitudes toward education, see LeRoy Craig Ferguson, *How State Legislators View the Problem of School Needs* (East Lansing, Mich.: Cooperative Research Projects, Michigan State University, 1960), Project No. 532.

[8] David Easton, *A Systems Analysis of Political Life* (New York: John Wiley, 1965). For an expansion of this model into a more elaborate systems approach, see Bertram M. Gross, "The State of the Nation: Social System Accounting," in *Social Indicators,* ed. Raymond A. Bauer (Cambridge, Mass.: The MIT Press, 1966), pp. 154–271.

[9] Terms comparable to "environment"—and used almost interchangeably with it—include "ecology" and "socioeconomic (or sociopolitical) context." For an

of a state legislative system in terms of state, federal, and local characteristics in order to discover why any given educational outcome results. After all, these ecological and political variables constitute the substratum within which a legislator must operate in setting policy.

In considering the state legislature generally we must take into account the activities of both federal and local officials as indicating overt demands or supports (or both).[10] Furthermore, once these inputs enter the legislature, we must study the interaction and processing that occurs to convert them into legislative outcomes. This conversion process constitutes the "within-put" phase of Easton's model, occurring in what he sometimes refers to as the "black box."[11]

Thus, the state legislature we regard as the arena for the interaction of "within-puts." As John C. Wahlke and his colleagues point out,[12] the state legislators provide structural regulation in response to the demands arising within their own separate collectivities, regarding such self-regulation as an integral part of their role. According to this conception, the legislator's role consists in converting the demands of his constituency, political party, friends, family, and various interest groups into a series of policies that are then considered as new objects of contention within the political community.[13] The main question is, *How much influence does the legislator actually wield during this conversion process?* Richard I. Hofferbert contends that the legislative arena—the "black box"—remains at present the most significant area of the field inviting further exploration.[14]

In addition to studying legislators, we should devote some of our

---

exposition of the trials of "ecology" as a concept in social science, see Otis Dudley Duncan, "Social Organization and the Ecosystem," in *Handbook of Modern Sociology*, ed. Robert E. L. Faris (Chicago: Rand McNally, 1964), pp. 76–78.

[10] See Easton, *A Systems Analysis of Political Life*, pp. 159–64.

[11] *Ibid.*, pp. 55–56.

[12] John C. Wahlke, William Buchanan, Heinz Eulau, and LeRoy Craig Ferguson, *The Legislative System* (New York: John Wiley, 1962), pp. 6–7.

[13] *Ibid.*, p. 253; and Easton, *A Systems Analysis of Political Life*, pp. 130–39. For a discussion of the variety of roles the legislator must play, see Wahlke *et al.*, *The Legislative System*, p. 14.

[14] Hofferbert, "Ecological Development and Policy Change," p. 465.

attention to examining interest groups. Like political parties, these exist to promote the aggregate and specific interests of their particular constituencies. By combining the demands placed on legislators, thus reducing them in number, these groups may ease the stress placed on legislators.[15] The latter usually have the advantage in dealing with interest group representatives since normally they do not have to support a particular interest to be reelected. Nevertheless, legislators often count on lobbyists to provide them with useful information to minimize their uncertainty on complex issues. This informational function is a central feature of the lobbyist-legislator relationship. The conception of the pressure group's entering directly into the legislative process is derived from the older political parties model that condoned the coercion of the leader by his followers.[16]

Supplied with resources from the environment and influenced, however indirectly, by the activities of interest groups, the legislators convert these inputs into policy outcomes for the political system. These outcomes are determined by the peculiar combinations of aggregate resources (i.e., state revenues), interaction patterns (e.g., balancing of roles), and the personal ambitions and attitudes of the legislators.[17] Policy outcomes, then, represent the authoritative distribution of social and physical goods and services into economic and noneconomic forms. *Vis-à-vis* the legislature, these outcomes have both external consequences (representing the relative success of

[15] John C. Wahlke, Heinz Eulau, William Buchanan, and LeRoy Craig Ferguson, "American State Legislators' Role Orientations Toward Pressure Groups," *Journal of Politics* 22 (May 1960): 203–27. The authors offer evidence that legislators do *not* see interest groups as "aggregative." See also Easton, *A Systems Analysis of Political Life,* pp. 414–28. Other actors who perform the aggregator and articulator functions are the President at the federal level and governors generally at the state level. The former is discussed in Phillip Meranto, *The Politics of Federal Aid to Education in 1955: A Study in Political Innovation* (Syracuse, N.Y.: Syracuse University Press, 1967). The latter are treated in Louis H. Masotti, "Intergovernmental Relations and the Socialization of Conflict: Interest Articulation in the Politics of Education" (mimeographed paper presented at the 1967 Midwest Conference of Political Scientists, Purdue University, 27–29 April 1967).

[16] See Norman R. Luttbeg, *Public Opinion and Public Policy: Models of Political Linkage* (Homewood, Ill.: The Dorsey Press, 1968), pp. 4–6.

[17] Easton, *A Systems Analysis of Political Life,* pp. 432–33.

particular programs or group demands) and internal repercussions (affecting, for example, legislators' interactional patterns and attitudinal configurations). Alternatively, we may regard the outputs as functional requisites of the political system that engender feedbacks that in turn supply system supports. The supports maintain the political system even though the demands effectuate changes in the conversion processes within the system.

This input-output model (or related derivations) has been used by Thomas R. Dye to study the policy outcomes of the American states[18] and by John C. Wahlke and his associates to study the roles of the state legislator.[19] Writers on economic development have generally focused on the relationships between industrialization, urbanization, wealth, and education on the one hand and political integration, political development, and public policy outcomes on the other.[20]

However, scholars have made little attempt to develop studies cutting across states or nations. This lack of comparative analysis has been decried by Phillips Cutright at the national level[21] and has been only partially remedied by Herbert Jacob and Kenneth Vines at the state level.[22] Thomas Dye and Ira Sharkansky have approached the comparative state study primarily from one level, emphasizing the use of aggregate indicators. Therefore, the input-output model receives undue attention at one data level while the "within-puts" of the model are to a large extent neglected. An attempt to remedy this oversight and to deal with the interaction between legislators and lobbyists has recently been made by Harmon Zeigler and Michael

[18] Dye, *Politics, Economics, and the Public,* p. 4.

[19] Wahlke *et al., The Legislative System,* pp. 17–28.

[20] In addition to Dye, writers who have taken this approach include Seymour M. Lipset, *Political Man* (New York: Doubleday, 1960); Robert Alford, *Party and Society* (Chicago: Rand McNally, 1963); and Lyle W. Shannon, "Is Level of Development Related to Capacity for Self-Government?" *American Journal of Economics and Sociology* 17 (1958): 367–82.

[21] Phillips Cutright, "Political Structure, Economic Development, and National Security Programs," *American Journal of Sociology* 70 (1965): 537–48.

[22] Herbert Jacob and Kenneth N. Vines, eds., *Politics in the American States: A Comparative Analysis* (Boston: Little, Brown, 1965).

Baer.[23] Their study, which builds on the earlier findings of Wahlke and associates,[24] partially bridges the gap between inputs and outputs.

Model 1:   The Economic Model

How relevant are legislators' opinions and attitudes to the determination of policy outcomes? This question must be posed if one is to take seriously the conclusions of economic determinists. The general systems model often used by these writers (see Figure 1–1) conceives

Figure 1–1   The General Systems Model

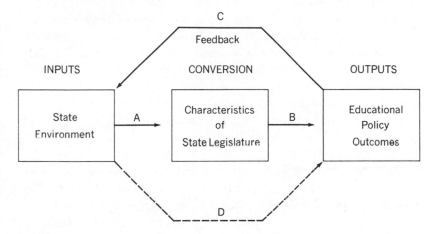

resources as inputs (supports and demands) that are converted, through the medium of legislative institutions and procedures (within-puts), into outputs (legislation) for the political system and environment. The policy outcomes have consequences for the citizenry that produce new considerations for the system, which may be regarded as feedbacks (linkage C).

[23] Harmon Zeigler and Michael Baer, *Lobbying: Interaction and Influence in the American State Legislature* (Belmont, Calif.: Wadsworth, 1969).

[24] Wahlke *et al., The Legislative System,* pp. 17–20.

The economic determinists, for whom Dye is a leading spokes-man, assert that there is a direct link (represented as *D*) between the inputs and outputs of the model. Conceived in this fashion, the model may be likened to a machine that ingests demand inputs and expels outputs *almost irrespective of the views of legislators.* We believe that this conception is inaccurate. But the question remains, In what ways and with what strength do the legislators enter into the policy-making process?

Incremental changes in expenditure levels, according to Ira Sharkansky, are a mediating influence between inputs and outputs. He believes that legislators, while not the primary converters of de-mands, nonetheless can and do make marginal adjustments in the conversion mechanisms.

Undeniably, prior allocations are an important factor in all budgeting situations. Nevertheless, the really significant question might be why the increment is as large or small as it is rather than why it is a change over the previous allocation. The incremental approach to policy making simply recognizes that populations change gradually and that short-run changes tend to be marginal; in other words, that a continual readjustment between population needs and policy outputs is both necessary and inevitable over time.

We are concerned in this study not only with defining the rela-tionships between ecological variables and educational outcomes, as Dye does, but also with exploring the considerations of incrementalism suggested by Sharkansky. In effect, we are attempting to answer the following question: If an educational outcome is closely related to (say) income, partisanship, and urbanization in one time period, will it be related to these same variables in the next time period?

We may facilitate our examination of the environment and its relationship to educational outcomes by taking two steps. First, by means of factor analysis, we can associate certain educational out-comes with other patterns of variables. Second, by means of stepwise multiple regression techniques, we can discover the order of im-portance of these variables to a given educational outcome.

Using factor analysis to bring order out of a congerie of diverse, seemingly unrelated variables has been best demonstrated by Richard

I. Hofferbert[25] and John Grumm.[26] In his research Hofferbert discovered that over time (1890–1960) an "industrialization" factor emerged that was defined by "patterns of economic and occupational activity."[27] Components of this industrialization factor included the Negro percentage of the population, per capita personal income, the urban percentage of the population, and the number of telephones per 1,000 population. Indeed, factor analysis revealed that from a vast assortment of variables certain patterns and combinations constantly recurred over time. Though Hofferbert found that the relationship between "industrialization" and educational expenditures varied substantially from one decade to another,[28] we may nonetheless reasonably expect to find comparable patterns emerging for educational variables.[29]

While considering many more variables than Hofferbert, Grumm also used factor analysis to detect patterns among his variables. While Hofferbert related his factors to various policy outcomes, Grumm chose to relate them to an index measuring state legislative "professionalism."[30] Apparently, one's choice of dependent variables for in-depth analysis is a function of the questions one wishes to answer. Hofferbert wished to talk about consistent variable patterns in relation to public policy whereas Grumm preferred to discuss the professionalism of state legislatures. We wish to consider the relative importance of different types of variables in relation to educational outcomes.

In approaching our subject we are especially conscious of Grumm's observation that prior studies

> have been concerned with policy output that could readily be quantified, and . . . almost all of this quantification has been based on

[25] Richard I. Hofferbert, "Socioeconomic Dimensions of the American States: 1890–1960," *Midwest Journal of Political Science* 12 (August 1968): 401–18.

[26] John Grumm, "Structural Determinants of Legislative Output" (mimeographed paper presented at the Conference on the Measurement of Public Policies in the United States, University of Michigan, Ann Arbor, Michigan, 28 July–3 August 1968).

[27] Hofferbert, "Socioeconomic Dimensions of the States," p. 411.

[28] *Ibid.,* p. 415.

[29] *Ibid.,* p. 416.

[30] Grumm, "Structural Determinants of Legislative Output," pp. 26–38.

financial indicators. It is not terribly surprising to discover that financial indicators of policy are sensitive to economic variables. In view of the nature of the data, the correlations of structural and political variables with these policy indicators, although possibly weaker, seem less trivial than those of economic variables with policy.[31]

In other words, although we may have greater difficulty explaining noneconomic educational outcomes than economic ones, we should not for that reason avoid investigating noneconomic variables or determinants. We should study noneconomic outcomes, which reflect the clash of social forces, equally as diligently as we do the highly visible, yet static, economic outcomes.[32] In this inquiry we shall examine both types of outcomes, economic and noneconomic.

In respect to previous aggregate studies of the fifty states, Ira Sharkansky has shown that regional patterns of expenditure exist in the United States.[33] One might disagree with his geographical divisions, but one could scarcely deny that regional differences do exist. We propose to test whether Sharkansky's conclusions apply to educational expenditures in the following manner. First, we will divide the nation into several regions and designate a pair of neighboring states within each region for the purposes of comparison; next, we will compare the two states on a variety of educational outcomes; finally, we will compare the four regions on these same outcomes, attempting to identify patterns or differences among them.

Is there any foolproof method for logically designating regions? Regionalism may be based on a variety of factors—common historical experiences, geographical compactness, and economic similarities, among others.[34] Scholars consistently disagree on the proper criteria for designating regions and rarely agree on even the number of regions, much less their composition. Any regional breakdown must

[31] *Ibid.,* p. 38.

[32] See Bertram M. Gross, "The State of the Nation," pp. 154–271; and Raymond A. Bauer, "Social Indicators and Sample Surveys," *Public Opinion Quarterly* 30 (Fall 1966): 339–49.

[33] Ira Sharkansky, "Regional Patterns in the Expenditures of American States," *Western Political Quarterly* 20 (December 1967): 955–71; idem, *Spending in the American States.*

[34] Daniel J. Elazar, *American Federalism: A View from the States* (New York: Crowell, 1966), pp. 79–116.

inevitably be somewhat arbitrary, and ours is no exception. We have divided the United States into four regions—the Northeast, the South, the Mountain West, and the Pacific Northwest—and have selected two states in each region for further analysis; these are, respectively, Massachusetts and Connecticut, North Carolina and South Carolina, Utah and Arizona, and Oregon and Washington.[35]

We have chosen four of these states for even more detailed analysis. If we can show that Massachusetts, North Carolina, Utah, and Oregon represent their respective regions and the fifty states generally, then we may legitimately extrapolate our findings in these states to the United States as a whole. Similarly, if we find that political variables help to explain resource allocation in the fifty American states, then we may infer that a close-up view of these states' experiences will probably be helpful in explaining legislators' roles in the allocation process. One aim of this study, let us reiterate, is to help to build a theory of the allocation of resources. Thus, if our first model, the economic model, should prove inadequate in explaining allocations, it is incumbent upon us to devise another model to explain educational policy making. This we have chosen to call the legislative model.

Model 2:   The Legislative Model

At this juncture our point of reference shifts slightly. Variables we earlier considered important to the determination of outcomes now become relevant to the interactions among legislators and their relations with lobbyists and constituents. This model may be likened to a series of spheres in which the inputs from any sphere actually originate in the larger spheres of which they are a part (see Figure 1–2).

[35] For analyses of the politics of these states, see Harvey S. Perloff et al., *Regions, Resources, and Economic Growth* (Baltimore: Johns Hopkins University Press, 1962); Elazar, *American Federalism;* V. O. Key, *Public Opinion and American Democracy* (New York: Alfred A. Knopf, 1961); Morris E. Garnsey, *America's New Frontier: The Mountain West* (New York: Alfred A. Knopf, 1950), pp. 10–58; Frank H. Jonas, ed., *Western Politics* (Salt Lake City: University of Utah Press, 1961); John H. Fenton, *Midwest Politics* (New York: Holt, Rinehart & Winston, 1966); and Duane Lockard, *New England Politics* (Princeton, N.J.: Princeton University Press, 1959).

Figure 1–2   Overlapping of Spheres in Models

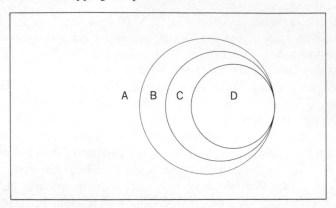

Sphere B in Figure 1–2 encompasses all the activities within sphere C; moreover, the characteristics of both B and C are circumscribed by the environment, A. Occasionally, sphere C may actually be a microcosm of A and B.

Relating this schema to our materials, we would suggest that the state legislature (represented as C) generally reflects the character of the political system (B) as well as that of the environment as a whole (A). Variables at large in the environment become specific system variables within the legislature and help to shape new outcomes, which in turn shape the environment.[36] Patterns of interaction within the legislature may be studied at one level of analysis and demographic variables and attitudes at another.

The individual state legislator (represented as D) is at the focal point of the legislative model. Although his characteristics may be determined empirically without referring to other individuals, his behavior is inevitably influenced by the actions of his colleagues and associates and by the demands of the environment. For example, although a legislator's choice of party is an individual matter, we find that in the legislature his choice materially affects his votes and interactions with peers and interest groups.

[36] The use of summary variables for individual indicators is examined by John M. Orbell (with Kenneth S. Sherill), "Racial Attitudes and the Metropolitan Context: A Structural Analysis," *Public Opinion Quarterly* 33 (Spring 1969): 47.

Not only partisanship but also party competition and urbanization have been found to affect legislators' attitudes and behavior toward interest groups and public policy. Even Thomas Dye, an acknowledged economic determinist, admits in his study of educational policy outcomes that significant associations

> exist between partisanship and elementary teacher preparation, pupil-teacher ratios, dropout rates, mental failures, the size of school districts and the extent of state and federal participation in school financing. The coefficients for these relationships are noticeably reduced when economic development is controlled, but we cannot reject the idea that there is some linkage between partisanship and these outcomes, a linkage which is not an artifact of economic development.[37]

In making this admission, Dye is merely reiterating the contention of Richard Hofferbert that outcomes must ultimately be considered in the light of interactions within the legislature.

Fortunately, our data will allow us to discuss both legislator-lobbyist interaction and legislators' perceptions regarding the power of education lobbyists. These variables are a portion of the attitudinal variables that we treat (generally, as dependent variables) throughout this analysis. We have asked legislators in four states (Massachusetts, North Carolina, Utah, and Oregon) a series of questions that probe their attitudes on educational issues, education lobbyists, and the legislative process; in addition, we have obtained from these legislators such conventional demographic data as their age, party affiliation, educational background, income, and occupation. We would not be surprised to find that one's party affiliation and his perception of pressure by education lobbyists might, when added to the traditional variables, help to explain the divergent views of legislators and lobbyists concerning the legislative process.[38]

[37] Dye, *Politics, Economics, and the Public,* pp. 107–8.

[38] The importance of linking leaders and followers at an elite-mass (or at an interest group leader-group member) level is amply supported by Norman Luttbeg and Harmon Zeigler, "Attitude Consensus and Conflict in an Interest Group," *American Political Science Review* 60 (September 1966): 655–66; Roberta S. Sigel and H. Paul Friesma, "Urban Community Leaders' Knowledge of Public Opinion," *Western Political Quarterly* 18 (December, 1965), 881–95; and Herbert McClosky, "Consensus and Ideology in American Politics," *American Political Science Review* 58 (June 1964): 361–82.

We regard this attempt to link different types of variables to one another as a potentially important contribution to the literature on the "funnel of causality."[39] The funnel of causality provides a simple paradigm for our second model, the legislative model, in that it suggests movement from the environment as a whole to the interaction within the legislative context, from there to the attitudinal configurations of the legislators, and finally to their votes on educational issues.

Education as a Subject for Political Inquiry

Our choice of education as a special area of concern to political scientists can be easily justified. "Education is perhaps the most important function of state and local governments," noted the Supreme Court in deciding the landmark case of *Brown* v. *Topeka* in 1954.

> Compulsory school attendance laws and the great expenditures for education both demonstrate our recognition of the importance of education to our democratic society. It is required in the performance of our most basic public responsibilities, even service in the armed forces. It is the very foundation of good citizenship. Today it is a principal instrument in awakening the child to cultural values, in preparing him for later professional training, and in helping him to adjust normally to his environment. In these days, it is doubtful that any child may reasonably be expected to succeed in life if he is denied the opportunity of an education.[40]

In this study we shall examine over time the aggregate behavior of the fifty states in relation to certain educational outcomes. In addition, we shall study the dynamics of the allocation process within four selected state legislatures.

[39] Angus Campbell, Philip E. Converse, Warren E. Miller, and Donald E. Stokes, *The American Voter* (New York: John Wiley and Sons, 1960), pp. 24–33; Robert T. Golembiewski, William A. Welsh, and William J. Crotty, *A Methodological Primer for Political Scientists* (Chicago: Rand McNally, 1969), pp. 396–419.

[40] *Brown* v. *Board of Education of Topeka, Kansas*, 347 U.S. 483 (1954), in Robert E. Cushman and Robert F. Cushman, *Cases in Constitutional Law*, 3d ed. (New York: Appleton-Century-Crofts, 1968), p. 1046.

A Preview

Hereafter follows an outline of the remaining chapters.

Chapter 2—Data: Theory, Sources, and Methodology

The object of this chapter is to describe to the reader the nature of our data and its arrangement in this book. We have divided our data into six major categories of variables: global, structural, and analytical for collectivities; absolute, relational, and contextual for individuals. After a brief description of these categories we discuss our choice of variables and their sources. Next we acquaint the reader with the content of the three attitudinal indices that we have created specifically for this study, namely, the educational issues index, the education lobbyist index, and the legislative process scale. Lastly, we explain the methods and techniques applied to the various types of data, thus clearing the way for an exposition of our first model.

Chapter 3—Model 1: The Economic Model

In this chapter we test whether economic variables determine all educational outcomes or whether some are in fact more closely related to political and social indicators. In addition, we explore the question of which variables enter the allocation equation after prior expenditures have been considered. Lastly, we attempt to determine whether earlier patterns of change are useful in explaining current patterns or in predicting future trends.

Chapter 4—Model 2: The Legislative Model

After testing the representativeness of our four states and noting the differences among the four regions, we attempt by means of factor analysis to explore and identify educational voting patterns in Oregon. We then relate various structural and demographic variables to the legislators' attitudes reflected in our three attitudinal indices. Among the structural (and related global) items considered are these: party affiliation; leadership status; degree of party competition, political incompatibility, and urbanization in the legislator's district; and the legislator's rate of interaction with lobbyists. The demographic variables discussed are the age, educational background, income, and occupation of the legislators in the four states. Lastly, we devote our conclusions to relating the several types of variables to one another.

Chapter 5—Consequences: A Review of Local Studies and a Perspective on the Future

We begin the final chapter by examining the current literature available on educational conflict at the local level and making suggestions for its improvement. Lastly, we summarize our findings in this study and make recommendations for future areas of research.

chapter 2

Data: Theory, Sources, and Methodology

Classifying the variables according to their common properties constitutes the first step in analyzing our data. Dependable data can materially enhance the credibility of theoretical models. By providing operational definitions for our models we can at least *begin* to build a theory of public policy making. Presently we will show what types of variables are applicable to our models.

Next we will devote a brief discussion to the sources of our data. Certainly an adequate data base is essential to thoroughgoing analysis. An unusual feature of this study is its concentration on secondary sources. The plea heard time and again for the better utilization of secondary sources has only rarely been heeded. Here we consciously attempt to show the usefulness of secondary studies.[1]

After we have classified the variables and reviewed our sources, we shall outline our analytic techniques. Examining our approach to the data thus constitutes the final preliminary prior to explicating our first model, the economic model. Although the study may seem

---

[1] An example of the rich potentialities of secondary studies is the work with case studies in Morris Davis and Marvin G. Weinbaum, *Metropolitan Decision Processes* (Chicago: Rand McNally, 1969).

technical, we have deliberately relegated much of the statistical analysis to appendices and summary tables. This organization of materials should help the reader to move more easily over the technical data and to grasp the thrust of the argument without devoting himself exclusively to technique.

Theory

How can we relate aggregate social and economic variables, as employed by Thomas Dye, to the attitudes and perceptions of state legislators, as explicated by John Wahlke and his colleagues? We attempt to bridge this chasm by means of the framework devised by Paul F. Lazarsfeld and Herbert Menzel. They suggest that with respect to collectivities three categories may be employed to describe behavior:

> analytical properties based on data about each member; structural properties based on the data about the relations among members; and global properties, not based on information about the properties of individual members.[2]

With respect to single individuals, however, Lazarsfeld and Menzel categorize variables as absolute, relational, or contextual. Absolute variables they define as "characteristics of members which are obtained without making any use either of information about the characteristics of the collective, or of information about the relationships of the member being described to other members," adding that "they thus include most of the characteristics used to describe individuals."[3] Absolute variables used in this study include the age, income, occupation, and educational background of legislators as well as their scores on various attitudinal scales.

In contrast to absolute variables, relational ones "are computed from information about the substantive relationships between the member described and other members."[4] Legislators' scores on

---

[2] Paul F. Lazarsfeld and Herbert Menzel, "On the Relation Between Individual and Collective Properties," in *Complex Organizations,* ed. Amitai Etzioni (New York: Holt, Rinehart & Winston, 1961), p. 426.

[3] *Ibid.,* p. 431.

[4] *Ibid.*

attitudinal scales can only be judged in relation to their colleagues' scores and to the beliefs that form the underlying dimensions of the scale. Similarly, on any index of opinion one's favorability or hostility toward an object or situation can only be measured in relation to others' views on the same subject. Relational variables may be legitimately linked with absolute and structural variables whenever we find the latter useful in explaining specific attitudes; in fact, we shall combine variables in this way in attempting to explain legislators' attitudes in our four selected states.

For a broader comparative analysis we may utilize contextual variables, defined as "properties which describe a member by a property of his collective."[5] For example, the factor scores for a state might well summarize the views of individual state legislators; similarly, the level of interaction between legislators and lobbyists might define the "pressure group" context of a state. The latter would constitute a contextual variable for the state that both legislators and lobbyists would have to take into account.[6]

The institutionalized interaction of legislators with interest groups is a *structural* characteristic of state legislatures generally.[7] This structural characteristic is to be distinguished from aggregate structural variables, which are based on a state's total population.

Obviously, variables are classified in accordance with the theories and judgments of researchers rather than in accordance with any definable empirical reality. Our own classification is intended to minimize the problems created by our use of several types of variables in the second model, the legislative model. This model embraces the levels of analysis in both Dye's and Wahlke's studies by its inclusion

[5] *Ibid.,* p. 433. The authors also define a "comparative property." We, however, use the comparative form as a process of inquiry throughout this study. Moreover, we believe that there are no variables in this study that would correspond to Lazarsfeld and Menzel's comparative properties. See *ibid.,* pp. 432–33.

[6] Allen H. Barton, "Bringing Society Back In: Survey Research and Macro-Methodology," *American Behavioral Scientist* 12 (November-December 1968): 5–9. See also James S. Coleman, "Relational Analysis: The Study of Social Organizations with Survey Methods," *Human Organization* 17 (1958–59): 30–31.

[7] It is among the "structural effects" noted by Ernest Q. Campbell and C. Norman Alexander, "Structural Effects and Interpersonal Relationships," *American Journal of Sociology* 71 (November 1965): 287–88.

of aggregate, structural, and personal (i.e., absolute and relational) variables.

In essence we are suggesting that a system of explanation that attempts to relate analytical (on the personal level, absolute and relational) variables and structural variables to global variables represents a feasible approach to the marriage of two research traditions. The analytical and structural emphasis of (for example) Wahlke's studies and the global emphasis of many recent policy analyses potentially represent, according to the Lazarsfeld-Menzel schema, complementary rather than contrasting approaches.

To simulate the context in which state legislatures operate, we have selected variables linking aggregate statistics to policy outcomes. Aggregate data not relating to individual legislators thus fall under the rubric of global data.[8] By reflecting environmental influences and characteristics peculiar to each state legislature, these data provide inputs that affect the individual legislators—constituting, in effect, contextual variables for particular legislatures. Thus, one piece of data might simultaneously be both a global variable for the legislature and (as a characteristic of the state) a contextual variable for the members of the legislature.

Sources

Thomas Dye has defined economic development as a complex involving "urbanization, industrialization, income, and the level of adult education."[9] These measures have often been linked to other global variables (e.g., the level of a state's educational expenditures) by various researchers. Confining one's analysis to a single type of

---

[8] The collectivity summarizes individual members' characteristics; thus, a group variable may parallel a personal variable. For example, although political affiliation is on one level a personal variable, the Democratic percentage of house membership may characterize an entire group of individuals and may be used in comparison with other summary or aggregate data. Lazarsfeld and Menzel, "Individual and Collective Properties," p. 430.

[9] Thomas R. Dye, "Policy Outcomes in Public Education" (paper presented at the Conference on Public Education, Center for the Advanced Study of Educational Administration, University of Oregon, 1966), p. 7.

variable makes explanation relatively simple and efficient whereas attempting to associate global variables with (for example) absolute variables entails the delicate task of explaining individual behavior.

One cannot presume to know individual legislators' attitudes strictly on the basis of policy outcomes. That is, in a state that spends large sums of money on education each legislator is not necessarily "favorable to education." Therefore, we would expect generally that in states exhibiting high levels of educational expenditures proportionately more legislators would be sympathetic to educational needs than in states with low levels of expenditures.

For the moment, let us examine what aggregate variables are available for our study and why they are important to the study of educational outcomes.

James A. Maxwell argues that interstate variations in educational expenditures are misleading in that the figures fail to include local expenditures.[10] Surely one must concede that local governments' contributions do have a significant impact on state allocations.[11] Similarly, the state's impact on local educational systems may be indicated by the proportion of school revenues (i.e., educational funds) that it provides. In addition, we might consider state and local taxes per capita as an important variable affecting state-local relations on educational financing. On a broader level and on the output side, we might examine the number of students per classroom and the per capita educational expenditures of both state and local governments. In fact, we have included all these variables in our analysis as indicators of state-local interaction.

As indicators of federal-state relations we have included as inputs such variables as the federal percentage of total welfare expenditures and federal grants to state and local governments per capita; as outcomes reflecting the political distribution of federal funds, we have included data on the specific disbursement of Vocational Act funds by state legislatures.

As general inputs we have included such variables as per capita income and Negro percentage of the population and as outcomes such

[10] James A. Maxwell, *Financing State and Local Governments* (Washington, D.C.: Brookings Institute, 1965), pp. 2–3.

[11] See John C. Wahlke, Heinz Eulau, William Buchanan, and LeRoy Craig Ferguson, *The Legislative System* (New York: John Wiley, 1962), pp. 342–76.

items as public school expenditures per pupil and per capita expenditures for higher education. In short, we have included in this study many of the variables used in the aggregate studies of Thomas Dye and John Grumm.[12] Our hope is that the outcomes studied here will reflect the interplay of inputs and within-puts. In order to add a temporal dimension to our analysis, we shall relate prior allocation patterns as inputs to certain educational outcomes.

At the aggregate level, then, we have borrowed most of our variables from the larger collections of Thomas Dye and John Grumm; these variables serve well to summarize the literature and data available at the present time. The use of large data banks was recently justified by Richard I. Hofferbert, who in defending his own selection of variables noted that

> the test of this particular list, either in terms of its cohesiveness or its inclusiveness, must be the same as for any alternative. Namely, how much promise does it hold for relating in a theoretically interesting manner to the dependent variables we seek to explain?[13]

This comment is neither flippant nor evasive: it merely takes cognizance of the wide variety of materials available. Incidentally, this same rationale may be used at the structural level—the "within-put" level—where we utilize the Democratic percentage of membership in the lower (and upper) house, the average winning percentage in gubernatorial elections, the Ranney interparty competition index, and per capita expenditures on the legislative branch (among other variables) as measures of linkages between inputs and outcomes.[14]

In addition to the foregoing, we have included structural variables relating to legislators' leadership roles, their rates of interaction with lobbyists, and the types of districts they represent. These indicators are meaningful only on a comparative basis, however; that is, interaction rates and measures of party competition and urbanization

---

[12] See Thomas R. Dye, *Politics, Economics, and the Public* (Chicago: Rand McNally, 1969), pp. 246–59; and John Grumm, "A Factor Analysis of Legislative Behavior," *Midwest Journal of Political Science* 7 (November 1963): 336–56.

[13] Richard I. Hofferbert, "Socio-economic Dimensions of American States: 1890–1960," *Midwest Journal of Political Science* 12 (August 1968): 407.

[14] Maxwell, *Financing State and Local Governments*, p. 2.

possess little meaning until we are familiarized with both their median levels and extremes. Moreover, these variables assume theoretical importance only when they are found to vary consistently with other specified variables. Many structural variables represent "face-sheet" characteristics that might be categorized in the following fashion:[15]

1. Power
    a. Leadership roles
    b. Political offices (past or present)

2. Contemporary status (achieved)
    a. Party affiliation
    b. Occupation

3. Legislative context
    a. Degree of urbanization in legislator's district
    b. Degree of party competition in legislator's district
    c. Legislator-lobbyist interaction rates
    d. Time allocations
    e. Techniques of lobbying

Of especial importance to this inquiry are the relational variables operative in the legislative arena.[16] Relational and structural variables may occasionally crosscut one another, just as structural and analytical features sometimes coincide in the same variable. Occupation, normally an analytical variable in that it constitutes the personal characteristic of a specific legislator, may take on relational qualities whenever it is used for comparisons within the legislature. Though proprietorship might generally be classified as an absolute variable (i.e., unique to each individual), once a proprietor becomes a legislator and is included in legislative studies, his occupational background retains significance only insofar as proprietor-legislators behave differently from other occupational groups within the legislature. Similarly, a lobbyist's representing business interests may have little

---

[15] Adapted from Hans L. Zetterberg, *On Theory and Verification in Sociology,* 3d ed. (New York: Bedminster Press, 1965), pp. 58–60.

[16] See Neal Gross, Ward S. Mason, and Alexander W. McEachern, *Explorations in Role Analysis* (New York: John Wiley, 1958), p. 51.

significance to researchers unless they can determine that legislators react differently to business lobbyists than to other lobbyists. If the latter point can be established, we might better understand the problems facing education and other lobbyists as compared to business lobbyists.

Absolute variables may include both demographic and attitudinal indicators. The demographic variables may be further subdivided as follows:

1. Contemporary status (ascribed)
   a. Age
   b. Number of years service (as a legislator or lobbyist)

2. Stratification
   a. Occupation (institutional classifications such as laborer, teacher, businessman, farmer)
   b. Income
   c. Organizational affiliations

3. Knowledge or expertise
   a. Years of schooling completed
   b. Degrees awarded

Demographic variables thus encompass the indicators most commonly utilized in studies of state legislatures, namely, age, income, educational background, and occupation.

In measuring attitudes we have decided to heed the advice of Robert T. Golembiewski and his colleagues about subjective scaling[17] and to use Guttman scale logic for our three attitudinal indices, which we have named the educational issues index, the education lobbyist index, and the legislative process scale. According to Guttman scale logic, a score of three on an itemized scale indicates that the respondent answered the *initial* three items (but not the fourth item) "correctly," but it gives no clue as to the responses subsequent to the fourth. A problem inherent to Guttman scale analysis is assuming an interval scale; the question inevitably intrudes, Does a scale score of four indicate twice the commitment or feeling as a score of two?

[17] See Robert T. Golembiewski, William A. Welsh, and William J. Crotty, *A Methodological Primer for Political Scientists* (Chicago: Rand McNally, 1968), pp. 412–19.

Table 2–1   A Comparison of Cornell Scores and Guttman Scale Scores
            for the Three Attitudinal Indices:
            Pearson Correlation Coefficient (r), Spearman's *Rho* (r_s),
            and Kendall's *Tau* (T)

	r	r_s	T
Educational Issues Index	.40	.31	.31
Education Lobbyist Index	.79	.77	.70
Legislative Process Scale	.90	.88	.86

NOTE: All correlations are significant at the .05 level or better.

In our own analysis we assume that the Guttman scale score differentiates respondents sufficiently to treat their scores as interval data whenever we use regression analysis. In fact, in comparing Guttman scale scores with Cornell scores (in which the respondent gets one point for each correct answer irrespective of the questions' order) we find that the two types of scores are significantly correlated (see Table 2–1) for our three attitudinal indices. Since the legislative process scale approaches perfect scalability, we use it throughout as an interval scale, whereas with both the educational issues index and the education lobbyist index we generally use the Cornell scores.

In Table 2–2 we have outlined the content of our three attitudinal indices and have listed the number of affirmative responses recorded for each question or statement in our interviews with 582 legislators in four states.

The educational issues index reflects legislators' attitudes toward the size of education budgets and tax support for education. Of the five questions, the one eliciting the greatest affirmative response related to the legislators' satisfaction with the previous year's education budget, and the one generating the least agreement related to perceptions of an increase in the proportion of expenditures for education. The other three questions verged between these two extremes in the responses accorded them. (In Chapter 4, incidentally, we will relate several structural and demographic variables to the responses on questions 2 and 5.)

On the education lobbyist index the greatest proportion of legislators agreed with the characterization of education groups as a "most

Table 2–2   Legislators' Responses on Items Comprising
           the Three Attitudinal Indices

	Affirmative Responses *N (of 582)*
Educational Issues Index (coefficient of reproducibility = .83)	
1. Do you feel satisfied with last year's education budget?	365
2. Would you favor a tax increase for education?	336
3. If your ideas on education budgets have changed, do you think that the budget should be larger?	228
4. If you were dissatisfied with last year's education budget, would you have preferred it to be larger?	142
5. Do you think that the proportion of expenditures for education will remain the same?	53
Education Lobbyist Index (coefficient of reproducibility = .77)	
1. Would you characterize education groups, including teachers' groups, as constituting a "most powerful organization"?	344
2. Did you, during the last year, often discuss educational matters with education lobbyists?	239
3. Do education lobbyists influence your votes on the education budget?	208
4. Do education groups, including teachers' organizations, apply the most pressure of any lobbyists?	153
5. Do you consider education lobbyists to be the best source of information on educational matters?	75
Legislative Process Scale (coefficient of reproducibility = .88)	
1. Legislators will talk to anybody who will bring really fresh information to their attention.	561
2. Interest groups and their agents give legislators valuable help in lining up support for their bills.	477

Table 2–2   (*continued*)

	Affirmative Responses N (*of 582*)
3. Under our form of government, every individual should take an interest in government *directly*— i.e., not through interest group organizations.	473
4. Legislators get valuable help in drafting bills or amendments from interest groups or their agents.	384
5. Lobbyists should have a greater voice in legislative decision making.	47

powerful organization," while the fewest number regarded education lobbyists as the best source of information on educational matters. Interestingly, not even a majority of legislators would agree that education lobbyists influence their votes on education budgets. With a coefficient of reproducibility of .77, this index is the weakest of our three attitudinal indices in its scalar form.

The legislative process scale ranges from the almost universal agreement among legislators that they constantly welcome fresh information, whatever its source, to the widespread view that lobbyists already have sufficient (if not excessive) power in the legislative process. While our two earlier indices focused specifically on education, this last scale is concerned with lobbyists generally and the legislative process.

What variables should be used to explain legislators' attitudes and the behavioral consequences of their attitudes (i.e., their votes)? We propose to use structural variables for this purpose.

To explain legislators' attitudes and votes, patterns of interaction with interest groups, party affiliation, and leadership status are among the structural variables most often chosen for this purpose by various researchers.

John Wahlke and his associates have analyzed legislators' relations with interest groups in terms of legislative leadership roles and attitudes toward pressure groups' influence in the political process.[18]

---

[18] John C. Wahlke, Heinz Eulau, William Buchanan, and LeRoy Craig Ferguson, "American State Legislators' Role Orientations Toward Pressure Groups," *Journal of Politics* 22 (May 1960): 203–27.

Duane Lockard has examined the importance of party affiliation to the legislator-lobbyist relationship in the New England states[19] and Harmon Zeigler and Michael Baer have done the same for Massachusetts, North Carolina, Utah, and Oregon.[20]

We will likely find that leadership position is not a key variable in explaining legislators' attitudes toward education. Heinz Eulau has observed that expertise is more commonly an attribute of rank-and-file legislators and of "challengers" to the leadership than of the leadership group itself.[21] Assuming that expertise is positively associated with support for education, one might conclude that factors other than leadership position would better explain educational attitudes. Samuel Patterson found that leadership roles, ideological (as distinguished from partisan) orientations, and personal characteristics were important in determining voting behavior in the Oklahoma and Wisconsin legislatures.[22] Malcolm E. Jewell has suggested that party affiliation helps to explain voting patterns in states characterized by strong party homogeneity while in other, less homogeneous states urban-rural, factional, and regional distinctions are more important.[23] In a state as heterogeneous as Oregon, to which our own voting analysis is confined, we would not expect party affiliation to be an important determinant of votes.

Legislative votes are important in that they indicate the distribution of legislators' preferences for the legislature as a whole. The totals tell us little or nothing about the relationship between individual legislators and the issue area; nor do they differentiate how individual votes were shaped by the general political environment. In this study we shall identify voting patterns on educational bills among the eighty-

[19] Duane Lockard, *New England Politics* (Princeton, N.J.: Princeton University Press, 1959), pp. 162–63.

[20] Harmon Zeigler and Michael Baer, *Lobbying: Interaction and Influence in American State Legislatures* (Belmont, Calif.: Wadsworth, 1969), pp. 112–14.

[21] Heinz Eulau, "Bases of Authority in Legislative Bodies," *Administrative Science Quarterly* 7 (October 1962): 309–21.

[22] Samuel Patterson, "Legislative Leadership and Political Ideology," *Public Opinion Quarterly* 27 (1963): 399–410.

[23] Malcolm E. Jewell, *The State Legislature* (New York: Random House, 1962), p. 75. For a discussion of partisan influences in Pennsylvania, see Frank J. Sorauf, *Party and Representation* (New York: Atherton Press, 1963).

four Oregon legislators by means of roll-call analysis of nonunanimous votes and shall attempt to relate legislators' individual scores (factor scores) within each pattern to various global, structural, and analytical variables. Thus, we shall treat votes both as absolute variables and as structural variables influenced by the interactions among legislators.

In analyzing roll-call votes in California, William Buchanan eliminated from his analysis any vote that drew less than 10 percent opposition in both houses of the legislature.[24] In our own analysis we have deliberately excluded unanimous educational bills and have added bills that encountered more than 10 percent opposition. Of the original seventy-eight bills, twenty-nine were considered for further analysis.

We did not weight these bills; nor did we pair votes, as did Buchanan. Instead, we utilized factor analysis (as suggested by Lee F. Anderson and his colleagues[25]) to identify blocs and coalitions. Since we expected that party and urban-rural distinctions would differentiate various types of legislators, we subdivided our sample as follows:

I. Senate
    A. Republicans
       1. Urban
       2. Rural
    B. Democrats
       1. Urban
       2. Rural

II. House
    A. Republicans
       1. Urban
       2. Rural
    B. Democrats
       1. Urban
       2. Rural

[24] William Buchanan, *Legislative Partisanship: The Deviant Case of California* (Berkeley, Calif.: University of California Press, 1963), pp. 152–53.

[25] Lee F. Anderson, Meridith W. Watts, Jr., and Allen R. Wilcox, *Legislative Roll-Call Analysis* (Evanston, Ill.: Northwestern University Press, 1966), pp. 123–74.

Using factor scores, we were able to determine the extent to which these groupings remained intact after being subjected to analysis.[26] In addition, factor analysis revealed the extent to which the various subissue areas of education are grouped in legislators' perceptions, as well as the makeup of these groupings.

Here let us briefly recapitulate our approach to sources. Originally, aggregate data for the fifty states collected by Thomas Dye, John Grumm, and ourselves encompassed more than 275 variables—a number that we had to reduce in order to consider the data in greater detail. We accomplished this reduction by means of factor analysis. In the final reduction we added educational variables such as the various allocations made under the 1963 Vocational Education Act, educational innovations, and membership in the American Federation of Teachers and the National Education Association. Factors thus identified were subjected to regression analysis in order to obtain predictive equations related to educational outcomes. Furthermore, for certain educational outcomes identified in the factor analysis we gathered additional data to make comparisons over time.

Next we applied the regression equations to data from our four selected states and from our neighboring control states to gauge the representativeness of our sample. Oregon, for example, was paired with Washington to determine whether the two states allocate resources for education in a roughly comparable manner. Pairing the states in this way enabled us to confirm the regional representativeness of the four states selected for analysis. Finally, we used a voting analysis of Oregon legislators to ascertain the linkages between various global, structural, and analytical indicators in relation to legislators' educational attitudes and votes.

The survey data available for Massachusetts, North Carolina, Oregon, and Utah are based on over twelve hundred interviews, 582 with legislators and 644 with lobbyists (see Table 2–3 for a breakdown by state). We have gathered the 84 Oregon legislators' votes on educational issues and, together with attitudinal and ecological data, have subjected these to regression analysis. We hope to draw some inferences for the fifty states from our original materials even though

---

[26] This general technique has also been used by Grumm, "A Factor Analysis of Legislative Behavior," pp. 336–56.

Table 2–3 The Legislator-Lobbyist Sample:
A Breakdown by State

	Legislators		Lobbyists	
	Number of Interviews Completed	Percentage of Legislators Interviewed	Number of Interviews Completed	Percentage of Lobbyists Interviewed
Massachusetts	244	87	185	100+*
North Carolina	164	97	132	100+*
Oregon	84	94	193	94
Utah	90	94	134	**

*Because some lobbyists failed to register (but were nonetheless readily identifiable and available), the number of interviews exceeded the number of registered lobbyists.
**Lobbyists do not register; no estimate possible.

they were gathered independently from the aggregate data derived from other sources. Fortunately, our four-state sample enables us to study interactional patterns among large groups of legislators and lobbyists on a comparative basis.[27] These data provide us the opportunity for extending knowledge and theory on the legislative determination of educational outcomes.

Methodology

Our methods vary according to the level of measurement we assume. Generally, we treat aggregate data as interval data. Therefore, we approach both the general political (input-output) model and the economic model through product-moment correlation and regression analysis, which comprise the multivariate statistics provided by factor analysis and multiple regression.

The legislative model employs both interval and ordinal data. Whenever possible, we explore linkages between different levels of measurement; in these cases, we compare the Pearson (product-moment) correlation coefficient with the Spearman (rank-difference)

---

[27] These data, which form the core of Chapter 4, were gathered by Zeigler and Baer and are analyzed in part in *Lobbying: Interaction and Influence in American State Legislatures.*

correlation coefficient and use the more conservative correlation for further analysis.

For our analysis of analytical (i.e., personal) variables and most structural variables we use statistics appropriate to the nominal and ordinal levels of measurement. Let us now consider in greater detail which statistics are appropriate for examining interval data and which are more suitable for studying nominal and ordinal data.

Interval Statistics

As earlier noted, we have over 275 variables available to us for each of the fifty states. How can we reduce these variables to coherent patterns for further analysis? We need a technique that will reduce the scope of the inquiry while enabling us to explore the most important and relevant data. We may accomplish this reduction by means of factor analysis[28]—more specifically, by means of the *R*-technique, which examines a collection of traits within a given population and calculates the underlying dimensions among the traits.[29] In other words, by means of the *R*-technique we can reduce the aggregate characteristics of the fifty states to a small number of factors that represent summary statements about the relationships among the states. After the reduction the factors are rotated to produce the simplest structure among the variables by the "varimax" criterion.[30] Futhermore, we can assign each state an "idealized score" (factor score) that sums up the original variables by the weight on the

[28] For a general discussion of factor analysis and its uses, see R. J. Rummel, "Understanding Factor Analysis," *Journal of Conflict Resolution* 11 (December 1967): 448–51.

[29] See Raymond B. Cattell, "The Principles of Experimental Design and Analysis in Relation to Theory Building," in *Handbook of Multivariate Experimental Psychology,* ed. Cattell (Chicago: Rand McNally, 1966), pp. 70–85.

[30] This method of finding the simplest structure is "an iterative procedure that maximizes a function [and] is employed to determine a transformation matrix which, when used to post-multiply the original factor matrix, results in the rotated matrix. The function maximized . . . is the variance of the squared loadings of the factor columns." Benjamin Fructer and Earl Jennings, "Factor Analysis," in *Computer Applications in the Behavioral Sciences,* ed. Harold Broko (Englewood Cliffs, N.J.: Prentice-Hall, 1962), p. 254.

factor.[31] Factor analysis is commonly employed to analyze interval data, but it may also be applied to other types of data (such as survey data).[32]

Thus, a logical first step in our analysis is to locate specific educational outcomes within a particular milieu. As Desmond S. Cartwright notes in his study of ecological variables,

> exploratory factor analysis, even up through the replication to check and refine summaries, interpretation, or measures of factors, strategically precedes multiple regression analysis; for one useful question that might be asked of factor analysis is: What variables (and what measures) are worth putting into a regression analysis?[33]

Next, we can use multiple regression to extend our examination of aggregate variables. We may consider the educational variables associated with each factor as dependent variables within multiple regression equations. Regression equations may be used in either of two ways. First, the original or "raw" scores for each independent variable in the equation can be related to the dependent variables. Second, the independent variables may be equated so that each has a mean of zero and a standard deviation of one when applied to dependent variables to provide standardized regression coefficients.[34] One substitutes original data into the first type in order to predict a dependent variable, whereas the second type is usually used in path analysis.[35] In this study we use multiple regression to predict educa-

---

[31] *Ibid.*, pp. 260–62.

[32] See the applications of factor analysis in Bruce M. Russett, "Social Change and Attitudes on Development and the Political System in India," *Journal of Politics* 29 (August 1967): 483–504; and G. R. Boyton, Samuel C. Patterson, and Ronald D. Hedlund, "The Structure of Public Support for Legislative Institutions," *Midwest Journal of Political Science* 12 (May 1968): 163–80.

[33] Desmond S. Cartwright, "Ecological Variables," in *Sociological Methodology*, ed. Edgar F. Borgatta (San Francisco: Jossey-Bass, 1969), p. 176.

[34] For an example of this type of analysis in social science, see Terry N. Clark, "Community Structure, Decision-Making, Budget Expenditures, and Urban Renewal in 51 American Communities," *American Sociological Review* 33 (August 1968): 576–93.

[35] For examples of the second type, see Otis Dudley Duncan, "Path Analysis: Sociological Examples," *American Journal of Sociology* 72 (July 1966): 1–16.

tional outcomes for variables selected by means of stepwise regression. Stepwise regression proceeds as follows:

1. The first independent variable identified is the one that explains (correlates most closely with) the largest amount of variance in the dependent variable. The amount of variance explained is indicated by the square of the multiple correlation (R^2).
2. The next independent variable selected is the one that explains the most *additional* variance in the dependent variable after the previous variable and others available have been partialled out. This second variable adds to the multiple correlation an increment of additional variance explained.
3. The process of choosing variables continues until (a) all of the variance is explained ($R^2 = 100\%$), (b) the partial correlations approach 1.00, or (c) the addition of the next variable does not materially affect the percentage of variance explained.

During the analysis regression weights called unstandardized regression coefficients (b) and standardized regression coefficients (B) are computed for each variable. Representing the independent variables as x_1, x_2, x_3 . . . x_n and the dependent as y, the regression equation would read like this:

$$\bar{y} = b_1 x_1 + b_2 x_2 + \cdots b_k x_n + a \text{ (intercept)} + \epsilon \text{ (error)}$$

Thus we see that stepwise multiple regression is a technique whereby the redundancy of the variables is recognized and taken into account.[36]

[36] The standardized regression coefficients "indicate *how much change* in the dependent variable is produced by a standardized change in one of the independent variables when the others are controlled," Hubert M. Blalock, Jr., *Social Statistics* (New York: McGraw-Hill, 1960), p. 345. In the case where we would assume that (1) our dependent variable was unambiguously *caused* by the independent variables, (2) our equation is recursive with independent error, (3) these independent variables were uncorrelated with the error in the equation, and (4) no independent variable is dependent upon another variable, our standardized regression coefficient would be equal to what are known as "path coefficients," "standardized path coefficients," or "dependence coefficients," see Kenneth C. Land, "Principles of Path Analysis," in *Sociological Methodology*, ed. Edgar F. Borgatta (San Francisco: Jossey-Bass, 1969), pp. 12–14. In this matter, Arthur S. Goldberger has argued that regression adequately explains the causal model, see Goldberger, "On Boudon's Method of

Nominal and Ordinal Statistics

When two or more variables indicate an underlying dimension or are considered as rankings rather than as metric or interval data, we may appropriately use the ordinal statistics *gamma,* Spearman's *rho* (r_s), and Kendall's *tau* (T).[37] A scale or an index may be considered as either interval or ordinal data. When large samples are involved, however, we find (as did Sanford Labovitz[38]) that the correlations are not very different. Table 2–4 shows the close relationship between Pearson and Spearman correlation coefficients for the three attitudinal indices used in this study. The Pearson correlation coefficient, therefore, is incorporated into the regression analysis in the aggregate section of this study.

With nominal data we employ a *lambda* (λ) statistic as the measure to reduce errors attributable strictly to guessing.[39] When nominal variables are used with ordinal scales, we use the chi-square (x^2) statistic and the appropriate measures of association. Studies utilizing chi-square and other nominal and ordinal statistics are now commonplace in the social sciences.[40]

Measures of Significance and Definition of Scales

The factor analysis in this study is of such an exploratory nature that we use very high cut-off points in our correlation of the variables

Linear Causal Analysis," *American Sociological Review* 35 (February 1970): 97–101. For only a few variables the path coefficients and standardized regression coefficients are equal; yet rather than confuse the reader, we maintain the regression terminology throughout. See further the discussion by Robert A. Gordon, "Issues in Multiple Regression," *American Journal of Sociology* 73 (March 1968): 592–616.

[37] William L. Hays, *Statistics for Psychologists* (New York: Holt, Rinehart & Winston, 1963), pp. 641–58.

[38] Sanford Labovitz, "Some Observations on Measurement and Statistics," *Social Forces* 46 (December 1967): 151–60.

[39] For a general discussion of *lambda,* see Linton C. Freeman, *Elementary Applied Statistics: For Students in Behavioral Science* (New York: John Wiley, 1965), pp. 71–78; and Hays, *Statistics for Psychologists,* pp. 606–10.

[40] The chi-square statistic can be approximated by a technique found in Morris Zelditch, *A Basic Course in Sociological Statistics* (New York: Holt, Rinehart & Winston, 1966), pp. 280–83.

Table 2–4   A Comparison of Pearson and Spearman
Correlation Coefficients for the Three Attitudinal Indices

	Educational Issues Index		Education Lobbyist Index		Legislative Process Scale	
	r	r_s	r	r_s	r	r_s
Educational Issues Index	—	—				
Education Lobbyist Index	−.097*	−.096*	—	—		
Legislative Process Scale	.025	.017	−.136*	−.137*	—	—

*Significant at the .05 level or better.

included within factors. While a correlation of .27 is significant for a sample of fifty states on a two-tailed test, we required correlations of .40 or higher in selecting variables for further factor analysis. Moreover, because we desired to establish independent factors, we have generally eliminated variables that were significantly correlated with more than one factor pattern.

Our multiple regression analysis employs the multiple correlation coefficient (R) as the significant statistic. Depending on the number of independent variables available and the number included in the regression equation, we generally use the .05 level (the standard social science criterion) as the base point for determining significance. We will, though, note higher levels of significance whenever they occur. In other words, if we find a correlation between two variables sufficiently high that it would have occurred by chance only 1 percent (.01) of the time, we will note the latter figure in our analysis.

Normally, the .90 coefficient of reproducibility distinguishes scales from quasi scales.[41] Even so, sometimes it is necessary to use as

[41] Allen Edwards, *Techniques of Attitude Construction* (New York: Appleton-Century-Crofts, 1957), pp. 193–98.

scales indices whose coefficients are slightly lower (e.g., the legislative process scale, whose coefficient of reproducibility is .88). Scales are most useful for assigning unique scores to individuals for further analysis (i.e., the scale score of a person getting four items correct in order on a five-item scale can be used as interval data for further analysis), whereas index scores cannot so easily be used as interval data.

To summarize our progress to this point, in this chapter we have (1) classified our variables as analytical, structural, global, absolute, relational, or contextual; (2) reviewed our choice of variables and the sources of our data; and (3) discussed the analytic techniques appropriate to each type of data. We are now ready to explore more fully our first model, the economic model.

chapter 3
Model 1:
The Economic Model

According to the assumptions implicitly held by economic determinists, all one needs to know to predict current levels of educational expenditure are the current economic inputs and the prior patterns of expenditure. The economic model is depicted in Figure 3–1. Observe that in this diagram linkages *A* and *B*, which connect the inputs to the outputs by way of the legislative realm, have been subordinated to linkage *D,* which connects the two directly. This model deliberately downgrades the importance of the political system in determining educational policy outcomes while emphasizing the importance of economic variables. In this chapter we will show that the economic model is inadequate for explaining all educational outcomes and that other types of variables help to explain changes in educational allocations. Let us initiate our discussion by proposing several general hypotheses that may be suggestive.

1. Educational policy outcomes are not solely the product of economic variables, but of political and social variables as well.
2. For those educational outcomes that are closely associated with economic variables, family income and per capita income will be particularly important variables.

Figure 3–1 The Economic Model

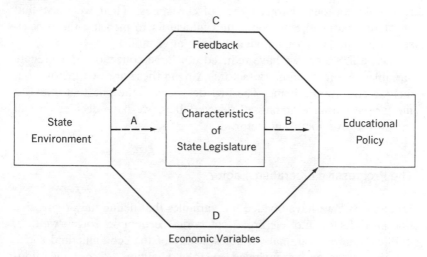

Economic Variables

3. Legislators in wealthy states will have more favorable attitudes toward education than those in poor states.
4. A legislature's decisions will be related to its members' attitudes.

Whenever legislators are not permitted the free exercise of their will, their votes may fail to reflect their attitudes, as, for example, when they are constrained by external forces. Overall, we would suggest that legislators' attitudes are an intervening (or conditional) variable between aggregate characteristics and policy outputs, just as structural and relational variables may be a potentially distorting force between a legislator's attitude and his vote. Thus, we may regard attitudes as propensities toward acting (i.e., voting) in a certain fashion that may sometimes be nullified by intervening variables. For example, as Robert L. Crain and Donald B. Rosenthal have demonstrated at the local level, highly educated policy makers are not necessarily friendly toward educational interests—either in their attitudes or in their voting practices.[1]

In attempting to provide empirical referents for our two models,

[1] Robert L. Crain and Donald B. Rosenthal, "Community Status as a Dimension of Local Decision-Making," *American Sociological Review* 32 (December 1967): 983–84.

we must first gather aggregate variables for the economic model that reflect the various characteristics of the states. Then we must find absolute, relational, and contextual indicators to measure the processes treated in the second model, the legislative model.

As a first step, we have reduced our large collection of aggregate variables to a few summary factors. Among these are two factors that include educational items. The broadest factor, the one that explains the largest variance among all the variables, we have decided to call the progressive liberalism factor.

The Progressive Liberalism Factor

In Table 3–1 we have divided the variables that define the progressive liberalism factor into five broad categories: economic, social, welfare, political, and educational variables. Many of the economic and social variables were earlier included in John Grumm's "economic affluence," "urbanization," and "welfare liberalism" factors.[2] Foreign and mixed parentage as a percentage of total population, per capita income, Negro percentage of the population, median school years completed, number of telephones per 1,000 population, and estimated market value of property per capita—all included in our first factor— were earlier found by Richard I. Hofferbert to be persistent indicators of "industrialization" and "cultural enrichment."[3]

Our progressive liberalism factor contains several original items that give it a welfare and political emphasis not found in previous studies. While including a few items borrowed from Grumm, the welfare category also includes measures of aid to dependent children, aid to the blind, and unemployment compensation, all three of which are positively related to the factor as a whole. In the political section

[2] John Grumm, "Structural Determinants of Legislative Output" (mimeographed paper presented at the Conference on the Measurement of Public Policies in the United States, Inter-University Consortium for Political Research, Ann Arbor, Michigan, 28 July–3 August 1968). This article is to appear in *Legislatures in Developing Perspective,* eds. Allan Kornberg and Lloyd Musolf (forthcoming).

[3] Richard I. Hofferbert, "Socioeconomic Dimensions of American States: 1890–1960," *Midwest Journal of Political Science* 12 (August 1968): 413.

Table 3–1　Components of the Progressive Liberalism Factor

	Factor Correlation
Economic Variables	
State and local taxes per capita, 1963: x_{41}	.84
State and local tax revenues per capita, 1961: x_8	.83
Median family income, 1959: x_{68}	.79
Retail sales per capita, 1963: x_{36}	.78
Per capita income, 1963: x_{32}	.72
Local tax revenues per capita, 1961: x_{84}	.70
State and local revenues per capita, 1961: x_{82}	.67
Estimated market value of property per capita, 1961: x_{31}	.60
Federal income and employment tax collections per capita, 1963: x_{40}	.55
Change in per capita income, 1950–60 (percentage of increase): x_{63}	−.49
Gini index, 1959: x_{111}	−.57
Social Variables	
Change in percentage of Negro population, 1950–63: x_{67}	.81
Cultural enrichment, Hofferbert factor, 1960: x_{113}	.79
Sound housing, percentage of total, 1960: x_{23}	.77
Median school years completed by persons over twenty-five, 1960: x_{22}	.75
Foreign and mixed parentage as a percentage of total population, 1960: x_{24}	.74
Number of telephones per 1,000 population, 1963: x_{29}	.73
College enrollment per 10,000 population, 1964: x_{23}	.54
Median age of population, 1960: x_{21}	.52
Per capita state expenditures for correctional system, 1961: x_{85}	.52
Paroled prisoners as a percentage of all releases, 1960: x_{110}	.48
Population per lawyer, 1963: x_{28}	−.56
Negro percentage of population, 1960: x_{20}	−.86
Draft board mental test, percentage of failures, 1963: x_{27}	−.89
Welfare Variables	
Aid to dependent children, average monthly payment per recipient, December 1964: x_{52}	.85

Table 3–1   (*continued*)

	Factor Correlation
Federal percentage of total welfare expenditures, 1961: x_{98}	.85
Old age assistance, average monthly payment per recipient, December 1964: x_{51}	.76
Unemployment compensation, average weekly payment per recipient, 1963: x_{54}	.72
Aid to the blind, average monthly payment per recipient, December 1964: x_{53}	.68
General assistance, average monthly payment per case, December 1961: x_{74}	.68
General assistance cases as a percentage of total population, 1961: x_{99}	.50
Per capita federal grants to state and local governments for health, welfare, and related activities, 1961: x_{81}	.41
Aid to the disabled, recipients per 100,000 population, December 1961: x_{107}	−.66
Aid to the blind, recipients per 100,000 population, December 1961: x_{108}	−.67

Political Variables

Democratic percentage of two-party vote for President 1964: x_{58}	.85
Party competition index for lower house, 1963–64: x_{13}	.75
Party competition index for senate, 1963–64: x_{12}	.68
Voter turnout in gubernatorial and senatorial elections in non-Presidential election years, 1952–60: x_{57}	.64
Democratic percentage of two-party membership in lower house, 1963–64: x_{16}	−.64
Percentage of membership in senate from majority party, 1954–62: x_{69}	−.70
Democratic percentage of membership in senate, 1963: x_{96}	−.79
Democratic percentage of membership in lower house, 1963: x_{95}	−.80
Ranney index of interparty competition, 1946–53: x_{17}	−.85
Average Democratic percentage in gubernatorial elections, 1956–62: x_{97}	−.86
Average winning percentage in gubernatorial elections, 1954–62: x_{70}	−.87

Table 3–1   (*continued*)

	Factor Correlation
Educational Variables	
Public school expenditures per pupil, 1963: x_{48}	.76
Per capita educational expenditures of state and local governments, 1961: x_{73}	.59
Educational innovation, 1966: x_{124}	.44
American Federation of Teachers membership, percentage of public school personnel in state, June 1966: x_{115}	.41
Percentage of Vocational Act funds allocated to adult education, 1965: x_{120}	.41

NOTE: Government budgetary figures are for fiscal years. See Appendix A for a complete listing of the variables subjected to factor analysis (number shown in subscript) and the data sources.

we find that voter turnout in non-Presidential election years, the Democratic percentage of the 1964 Presidential vote, and party competition in the state legislature (both chambers) are the only variables positively related to "progressive liberalism."

The social characteristics of the states are illuminated by such variables as parole policies, per capita expenditures for the correctional system, Negro population increase, college enrollment, the median age of the population, and the proportion of sound housing. All of these variables are positive correlates of the progressive liberalism factor.

Among the economic indicators, federal income and employment tax collections, retail sales, property values, the two income measures, and the four measures of state and local revenues are all positively related to "progressive liberalism." Only two economic variables are negatively related to the 'factor, namely, the unequal distribution of income (as measured by the Gini index)[4] and the change in per capita income for the period 1950–60. On the basis of these findings, we would hypothesize that states displaying a high *stable* level of income (in particular, Northern industrial states) would score highest on a

[4] The index figures used for each of the fifty states are available in Thomas R. Dye, "Income Inequality and American State Politics," *American Political Science Review* 63 (March 1969): 159.

scale measuring progressive liberalism, whereas poor states (in particular, Southern states) would be grouped at the bottom of the scale.

We may test this hypothesis by assigning factor scores to each of the fifty states according to their rankings on the fifty variables comprising the progressive liberalism factor. Table 3–2 shows the results of these computations. As expected, the wealthy industrial states of the North are concentrated at the high end of the scale, while the eleven states of the Old Confederacy are huddled at the bottom of the scale. Fortunately, the four states that we have chosen for more intensive analysis are scattered almost randomly throughout the scale: Massachusetts is first, Oregon eleventh, Utah twenty-fifth, and North Carolina forty-fifth in the rankings of the fifty states.

Lastly, the five educational variables included in the progressive liberalism factor are per capita educational expenditures of state and local governments, public school expenditures per pupil, American Federation of Teachers membership, percentage of Vocational Act funds allocated to adult education, and educational innovation. In addition to the foregoing, we will consider the state's percentage of total school revenues (i.e., outlays) as a dependent variable for further examination within the context of the progressive liberalism factor.

The Federalism-and-Concern Factor

Ten percent of the variance among all the variables originally gathered can be explained by our second factor, which (because of its constituent variables' emphasis on federal support and welfare expenditures) we have decided to call the "federalism-and-concern" factor. John Grumm's "legislative professionalism" factor is partially reflected by our two "legislative investment" items, while additional variables from his "federal support" factor are included within our "federal concern" category.[5]

We would expect that predominantly Democratic states that rely heavily upon federal funds and have high welfare commitments would have positive "idealized scores" on this factor. This generalization is

[5] Grumm, "Structural Determinants of Legislative Output," pp. 18–26. Our four states fall into different clusters of states within Grumm's "professionalism index." *Ibid.,* p. 27.

Table 3–2 Progressive Liberalism Factor Scores
for the Fifty States

State	Factor Score	State	Factor Score
Massachusetts	1.31	Pennsylvania	.30
Connecticut	1.22	Alaska	.28
Washington	1.16	Vermont	.27
Wisconsin	1.15	Hawaii	.23
New York	1.11	Delaware	.16
California	1.08	Idaho	.13
Colorado	.97	Maryland	.04
Iowa	.94	Maine	−.03
Minnesota	.94	Oklahoma	−.09
Illinois	.91	Missouri	−.25
Oregon	.90	Arizona	−.29
Kansas	.89	New Mexico	−.29
Rhode Island	.81	West Virginia	−.67
Michigan	.80	Kentucky	−.98
Nevada	.78	Texas	−1.00
North Dakota	.74	Tennessee	−1.25
Montana	.74	Virginia	−1.27
Wyoming	.73	Florida	−1.30
New Jersey	.73	Louisiana	−1.45
Ohio	.71	North Carolina	−1.64
New Hampshire	.65	Arkansas	−1.69
Indiana	.64	Alabama	−2.11
Nebraska	.48	Georgia	−2.12
South Dakota	.33	Mississippi	−2.84
Utah	.30	South Carolina	−2.88

undercut, however, by the extent to which the state has been generally innovative or has had large changes in agricultural value between 1950 and 1960. As Table 3–3 indicates, these two variables are negatively associated with federalism-and-concern scores.

Three educational variables emerge within the factor: per capita expenditures for higher education, the percentage of Vocational Act funds allocated to postsecondary education, and the number of students per classroom. Later in this chapter we will treat these as dependent variables and, by means of stepwise multiple regression

Table 3–3   Components of the Federalism-and-Concern Factor

	Factor Correlation
Legislative Investment: Political Variables	
Per capita expenditures on compensation of legislators, 1963–64 biennium: x_{10}	.82
Per capita expenditures on the legislative branch, 1963–64 biennium: x_8	.74
Federal Concern: Economic Variables	
Federal percentage of total educational expenditures, 1961: x_{72}	.84
Total federal expenditures per capita, 1963: x_{37}	.82
Federal defense expenditures per capita, 1963: x_{38}	.76
Federal grants to state and local governments per capita, 1963: x_{39}	.70
Percentage of state and local revenues from federal government, 1963: x_{43}	.52
State Concern: Welfare and Economic Variables	
State and local expenditures for welfare as a percentage of personal income, 1961: x_{86}	.90
State general revenues per capita, 1964: x_{44}	.65
Per capita state expenditures for correctional system, 1961: x_{85}	.45
Miscellaneous Variables	
Democratic percentage of two-party membership in senate, 1963–64: x_{15} (Political)	.95
Change in value added by agriculture, 1950–60: x_{64} (Economic)	$-.59$
General innovations: x_{123} (Social)	$-.60$
Educational Variables	
Per capita expenditures for higher education, 1963: x_{55}	.64
Percentage of Vocational Act funds allocated to postsecondary education, 1965: x_{119}	.44
Number of students per classroom, 1964: x_{50}	$-.82$

NOTE: Government budgetary figures are for fiscal years. See Appendix A for a complete listing of the variables and data sources.

48

Table 3–4 Federalism-and-Concern Factor Scores
for the Fifty States

State	Factor Score	State	Factor Score
Idaho	.605	Iowa	.180
Michigan	.605	South Dakota	.165
Maine	.547	North Carolina	.159
Utah	.545	Arizona	.106
Ohio	.526	Missouri	.103
Indiana	.489	North Dakota	.078
Kentucky	.437	Alabama	.073
Pennsylvania	.415	Florida	.066
New Jersey	.409	Oregon	.000
West Virginia	.363	Virginia	−.020
Minnesota	.351	Texas	−.026
New York	.342	Washington	−.033
Illinois	.336	Colorado	−.057
Wisconsin	.321	Wyoming	−.058
Georgia	.315	Maryland	−.103
New Hampshire	.293	Oklahoma	−.114
South Carolina	.282	Connecticut	−.127
Tennessee	.270	Montana	−.137
Mississippi	.259	Delaware	−.140
Rhode Island	.259	Massachusetts	−.205
Kansas	.246	New Mexico	−.409
Nebraska	.230	Nevada	−.425
Vermont	.200	California	−.522
Arkansas	.184	Hawaii	−.843
Louisiana	.180	Alaska	−6.721

techniques, will relate them to the other variables in the federalism-and-concern factor.

In ranking the states according to their scores on "federalism and concern," we find that no clear-cut regional patterns emerge (see Table 3–4). Again, however, our four selected states fall into different clusters in an almost random fashion: Utah is fourth, North Carolina twenty-eighth, Oregon thirty-fourth, and Massachusetts forty-fifth among the fifty states.

Hypotheses To Be Tested

Later in this chapter we propose to test a series of propositions relating to the educational variables identified with our two factors. In testing the propositions, we will regard the dependent variables as outputs, the economic, social, and welfare variables as inputs, and the political variables as within-puts. Let us here list the nine propositions and their corollaries that we will test.

PROPOSITION 1: *State educational allocations will be most closely associated with economic variables.*

> COROLLARY 1: *State educational allocations will be related only slightly to political and social variables.*

PROPOSITION 2: *Insofar as they do not require large expenditures of money, educational innovations will be more closely associated with political and social variables than with economic variables.*

> COROLLARY 2: *Insofar as educational innovations require large expenditures of money, they will be significantly related to economic variables such as per capita income.*

PROPOSITION 3: *Membership in the American Federation of Teachers will be greatest in areas that have previously been unionized (i.e., in urban, industrialized areas).*

PROPOSITION 4: *The percentage of Vocational Act funds allocated to adult education will be related primarily to political variables.*

PROPOSITION 5: *The state's share of educational outlays will be primarily associated with economic variables.*

> COROLLARY 5: *Whenever the state's share is not primarily a function of its wealth, it will be strongly dependent upon political variables.*

PROPOSITION 6: *Current educational expenditures will be strongly related to prior allocations.*

PROPOSITION 7: *Proposition 6 notwithstanding, current educational expenditures will be related to variables other than those associated with prior allocations.*

PROPOSITION 8: *Per capita expenditures for higher education (like other economic outcomes) will be most closely associated with economic variables.*

PROPOSITION 9: *The number of students per classroom will be most closely associated with political and social variables.*

Prior to discussing our own analysis and conclusions, let us briefly review previous researchers' findings pertinent to the educational variables identified in our two factors.

Some Perspectives on Educational Policy Outcomes

Currently the states are searching for new ways to involve the federal government in education, hoping thereby to lessen their own financial burden. The state governments are also trying to place an increasingly large share of the responsibility for education on local governments and are attempting to raise additional educational funds by resorting to increased sales taxes or other revenue sources. The success of these initiatives is in large measure a function of the individual state's wealth.

A state's support for education, according to Glen W. Fisher, is best understood in relation to its tax system, which in turn is partially shaped by the amount and distribution of financial resources among its residents.[6] Indeed, the variable most detrimental to the support of education and local school systems may well be a high percentage of families with incomes of less than $2,000 a year for these families neither contribute to the tax base nor have the wherewithal to participate meaningfully in the establishment of an exemplary educational system.

In explaining his choice of variables, Fisher notes that overlapping is necessary to discern the "best" item to explain a particular output and observes that "no single statistical series can adequately describe

---

[6] Glen W. Fisher, "Interstate Variation in State and Local Government Expenditures," *National Tax Journal* 17 (March 1964): 65.

the spatial distribution of population in a given state."[7] How are we to choose among the possible variables? Earlier we used factor analysis to reduce the number of variables to manageable proportions; later in this chapter we will use stepwise regression to choose the variables that contribute the best explanation of the variance in particular outcomes. While we offer previous studies as justification for using certain variables for further analysis, others we include because we are attempting to expand existing theory and to build new explanations. These new explanations are, of course, open to replication and secondary analysis—a step forward, we would assert.

Seymour Sacks and Robert Harris, while examining various state and local government expenditures in terms of the intergovernmental flow of funds, found that the allocations for both higher education and local schools were greatly dependent upon the level of per capita income within the states. After constructing regression coefficients explaining per capita general expenditures for local school districts, the authors concluded that per capita income is an important determinant of educational allocations.[8] Interestingly, at about the same time Jerry Miner found that the variables most closely related to per capita expenditures for education were personal income per capita and the proportion of students in the population.[9]

As suggested earlier in Proposition 1, we would expect economic educational outcomes such as public school expenditures per pupil to be closely associated with economic variables. Reviewing the literature, we find that James A. Kelly and his colleagues lend support to this view in their study of educational expenditures in large American cities.[10] They found that the variables most significantly related to

---

[7] *Ibid.*, p. 62.

[8] Seymour Sacks and Robert Harris, "The Determinants of State and Local Government Expenditures and Intergovernmental Flow of Funds," *National Tax Journal* 17 (March 1964): 75–85.

[9] Jerry Miner, *Social and Economic Factors in Spending for Public Education* (Syracuse, N.Y.: Syracuse University Press, 1963), pp. 100–3.

[10] H. Thomas James, James A. Kelly, and Walter I. Garms, *Determinants of Educational Expenditures in Large Cities in the United States* (East Lansing, Mich.: Cooperative Research Projects, Michigan State University, 1966), Project No. 2389.

public school expenditures per pupil were median family income and property value,[11] variables that we would expect to be prominent also at the state level.[12]

Other writers have found per capita income and median family income to be associated with educational expenditures in the various states.[13] Ira Sharkansky, in analyzing per capita educational expenditures, found that they were related most strongly to population growth. The percentage of adults with a college education, sales taxes per capita, sales taxes as a percentage of total tax revenues, the state's percentage of state and local educational expenditures, the percentage of revenues from nonlocal sources, the number of state employees per 10,000 population, and the previous expenditures on education were among the independent variables that were positively related to public school expenditures per pupil.[14]

While we might expect previous educational expenditures to be the most powerful variable affecting current state expenditures, we would also expect that at any given expenditure level political variables would determine the specific distribution of funds. Sharkansky, however, found that

> spending for education and welfare . . . shows fewer relationships with political characteristics than spending for other fields of service. Perhaps professional administrators in charge of state welfare and educational agencies are more isolated than other agencies' officials from the influence of parties and elected officials.[15]

[11] *Ibid.*, p. 110.

[12] A warning, however, on the difficulties of switching from one areal unit to another (e.g., from cities to states) is voiced by Otis D. Duncan, Ray P. Cuzzort, and Beverly Duncan, *Statistical Geography: Problems in Analyzing Areal Data* (Glencoe, Ill.: The Free Press, 1961).

[13] See Thomas R. Dye, *Politics, Economics, and the Public* (Chicago: Rand McNally, 1966), pp. 80–82.

[14] Ira Sharkansky, "Economic and Political Correlates of State Government Expenditures: General Tendencies and Deviant Cases," *Midwest Journal of Political Science* 11 (May 1967): 175–80.

[15] Ira Sharkansky, *Spending in the American States* (Chicago: Rand McNally, 1968), p. 69.

Wayne L. Francis lends support to Sharkansky's view, asserting that education is one of the legislative areas that is relatively free of politics.[16]

We would expect educational allocations, like most other allocations, to be incremental at the state level. Fluctuations in the proportion of school revenues contributed by the state will be determined by political variables external to the legislature. In other words, requests for educational funds will be the product of agency and interest group interaction outside the legislative context. As with other educational expenditures, we would expect Democratic political indicators to be related negatively[17] and party competition positively to the state's share of educational revenues.

In Gordon Cawelti's study of innovations in American schools, the author concluded that high per pupil expenditures, large enrollments, private secular schools, and urban and suburban (as opposed to rural) locales predominated among the school districts with the highest innovative rates.[18] Harmon Zeigler and Karl F. Johnson expanded on these data and concluded that educational innovations were most closely related to per capita income.[19] We would expect the relationship between wealth and educational innovation to emerge even in a broader pattern of variables.

With respect to the percentage of Vocational Act funds allocated to adult education, variables relating to federal assistance and party competition emerge as particularly important.[20] Bruce F. Davie and Philip D. Patterson, Jr., argue that the state legislators' disbursement of these funds is made with respect to the political culture of the state; i.e., the bulk of funds may be spent on buildings even though only a third of the money must, by law, be spent on educational programs or

[16] Wayne L. Francis, *Legislative Issues in the Fifty States* (Chicago: Rand McNally, 1967), pp. 48–49.

[17] See Dye, *Politics, Economics, and the Public,* pp. 258–67.

[18] Gordon Cawelti, "Innovative Practices in High Schools: Who Does What— and Why—and How," *Nations Schools* 79 (April 1967), 56–74.

[19] Harmon Zeigler and Karl F. Johnson, "Educational Innovation and Politico-Economic Systems," *Education and Urban Society* 1 (February 1969): 174–75.

[20] Bruce F. Davie and Philip D. Patterson, Jr., *Vocational Education and Intergovernmental Fiscal Relations in the Post-War Period* (Washington, D.C.: Georgetown University, 1966), pp. 76–84.

construction;[21] political decisions must inextricably be involved in the allocation process. We would expect that the proportion of Vocational Act funds allocated to educational facilities will be particularly high in Southern states.

Turning now to the last educational variable delineated in the progressive liberalism factor, let us review previous researchers' findings regarding membership in the American Federation of Teachers (AFT). As J. Douglas Muir has noted, while only 8 percent of American public school teachers belong to the American Federation of Teachers, a much smaller number than belong to the National Education Association,[22] the organization's membership has increased an average of 18 percent yearly since 1959, with the greatest growth occurring in cities.[23] Muir concludes that the growth of teacher unions is most pronounced in urban areas—as does also Stephen Cole in his study of the unionization of teachers.[24]

According to Cole, the factors most important in determining union membership and militancy are the number of men in the teaching system, the party affiliations of the teachers, their family background, the length of their experience within the school system, and a prior history of union membership in the family.[25] The point, of course, is that unionism has traditionally made greatest headway in urban, industrialized areas. We would expect to find AFT membership related to a pattern that included the proportion of foreign and imigrant stock in the working class population and other urban and social variables—variables that would likely not go very far in explaining membership in the comparatively stodgy National Education Association.

[21] *Ibid.,* p. 89.

[22] T. M. Stinnett, *Turmoil in Teaching* (New York: Macmillan, 1968), pp. 372–73. While the NEA is by far the largest single educational organization, the distribution of its membership did not appear in the progressive liberalism factor.

[23] J. Douglas Muir, "The Tough New Teacher," *American School Board Journal* 156 (November 1968): 14.

[24] Stephen Cole, "The Unionization of Teachers: Determinants of Rank-and-File Support," *Sociology of Education* 41 (Winter 1968): 66–87; see also Haakon L. Andreasen, "Teacher Unionism: Personal Data Affecting Membership," *Phi Delta Kappan* 50 (November 1968): 177.

[25] Cole, "The Unionization of Teachers," p. 87.

Turning now to the educational variables in the federalism-and-concern factor, we find that per capita expenditures for higher education are readily available for the years 1964 through 1966 in the *Statistical Abstract of the United States.*[26] At the outset we should note that researchers familiar with this subject area have consistently asserted that expenditures for higher education are not related to the same set of variables as other educational expenditures. Robert H. Salisbury claims that allocations for higher education are a part of the political process of the state in a way unlike other allocations.

> Public higher education bears little political relationship to elementary and secondary schools. In organizational structure, in methods of financing, and in the pressures and politics of decision-making, state colleges and universities are part of a different system from the schools.[27]

In a similar vein, M. M. Chambers advises researchers observing the rapid increase in state educational allocations to consider also the historical background of expenditures in relation to higher education.[28] Salisbury found that in North Carolina and Utah expenditures for colleges are high in relation to public school expenditures, whereas in Massachusetts college expenditures are relatively low in comparison to public school expenditures; in Oregon the two types of expenditures are proportionate to one another but high.[29] However, in recent years both Massachusetts and North Carolina have rapidly increased their public school allocations. Thus, we cannot easily identify trends unless we are able to specify the exact context relevant to the expenditures under investigation. Specifically, unless we know what variables are important in determining expenditures for higher education, we can deduce little from the information that Utah and North Carolina spend

[26] U.S. Bureau of the Census, *Statistical Abstract of the United States, 1968,* 89th ed. (Washington, D.C.: Government Printing Office, 1968), pp. 13 and 133.

[27] Robert H. Salisbury, "State Politics and Education," in *Politics in the American States,* eds. Herbert Jacob and Kenneth N. Vines (Boston: Little, Brown, 1965), p. 363.

[28] M. M. Chambers, "Current State Tax Support," *Phi Delta Kappan* 50 (October 1968): 113–16.

[29] Salisbury, "State Politics and Education," p. 362.

proportionately more on higher education than on elementary and secondary education. The variables affecting one type of educational expenditure may be completely different from those affecting another.

According to Salisbury's analysis, both local and state support for public schools correlate weakly with expenditures for higher education ($r = .39$ and $.28$, respectively). Noting that nonurban states are more favorably disposed toward the funding of higher education than one might expect, Salisbury concludes that allocations for higher education are relatively unrelated to income levels or to measures of party competition.[30] Glen W. Fisher, on the other hand, believes that measures of party competition help to explain the amount of resources allocated to higher education and that Democratic politics, when dominant, are negatively associated with expenditures for higher education.[31] Moreover, he asserts that federal grants-in-aid (for whatever purpose—welfare or elementary and secondary education), by freeing additional state fiscal resources, should correlate positively with state expenditures for higher education.

The number of students per classroom is an altogether different type of variable. According to Bruce F. Davie and Philip D. Patterson, Jr., variables positively associated with expenditures for higher education will be negatively related to the number of students per classroom.[32] We must remember that the number of students per classroom, unlike our other educational variables, denotes support or concern only insofar as its figures are *low* rather than high. Similarly, we can expect the variables associated positively with disbursements of Vocational Act funds to postsecondary education to be negatively related to the number of students per classroom. The provisions of the Vocational Education Act of 1963 required that at least one-third of all federal funds had to be used for construction or for postsecondary vocational education;[33] thus, a state was free to allocate the funds as it pleased, subject only to some very loose guidelines. We would expect, therefore, that the decisional processes that determine state

[30] *Ibid.*, p. 361.

[31] Fisher, "Interstate Variation in Government Expenditures," p. 66.

[32] Davie and Patterson, *Vocational Education and Intergovernmental Fiscal Relations*, p. 89.

[33] *Ibid.*, p. 84.

expenditures for higher education will be relevant to the Vocational
Act disbursements to postsecondary education as well.

A Multiple Regression Analysis
of Selected Educational Outcomes

How did all the expectations expressed in the previous section and in
our earlier hypotheses fare in the testing? Presently we shall subject
the eight educational variables identified with our two factors and
other related variables to multiple regression. Treating the educational variables as dependent variables, we shall derive a multiple
regression equation that relates each dependent variable to the other
independent variables in the factor in such a way as to explain the
greatest variance in the former. We shall examine the nine dependent
variables in the following order:

1. Per capita educational expenditures of state and local govern-
    ments.
2. Public school expenditures per pupil.
3. Percentage of school revenues from state.
4. Educational innovation.
5. Percentage of Vocational Act funds allocated to adult education.
6. American Federation of Teachers membership.
7. Per capita expenditures for higher education.
8. Percentage of Vocational Act funds allocated to postsecondary
    education.
9. Number of students per classroom.

Since we believe that existing theory suffers from an overemphasis
on economic variables (a condition attributable to the widespread
influence of the economic determinists), we will be emphasizing in
our own analysis the importance of political and social variables to
the determination of educational policy outcomes.

Per Capita Educational Expenditures of State and Local Governments

Contrary to expectations, variables relating to federal aid did
not materially add to our explanation of the level of state and local

educational expenditures per capita. Instead, we found that state and local revenues per capita was the variable most closely related to per capita educational expenditures of state and local governments in (fiscal) 1961—not only in terms of the simple correlation ($r = .869$) but also in terms of the standardized regression coefficient (see Table 3–5).[34]

A high median age and a high proportion of foreign and mixed stock among the population are dampeners on per capita educational expenditures. Similarly, the federal percentage of total welfare expenditures is negatively related to per capita educational expenditures, as are four other variables (change in per capita income from 1950 to 1960, American Federation of Teachers membership, party competition in state senates, and Vocational Act disbursements to adult education) to a lesser extent. On the other side, both median family income and population per lawyer are positive correlates but are not nearly so important as the proportion of the population enrolled in college and state and local revenues per capita.

In Tables 3–6 and 3–7 we have listed the variables most closely associated with per capita educational expenditures of state and local governments for (fiscal) 1965 and 1966, respectively. These two time periods share a common background of prior allocation; that is, 1965 educational expenditures are primarily determined by the comparable expenditures for 1961, as are likewise the 1966 figures dependent upon those for 1965. These data lend credence to Sharkansky's argument that prior expenditures must be considered of primary importance to current expenditures rates,[35] further illustrating the incremental nature of legislative action.

In Table 3–6, as expected, we find that per capita educational expenditures of state and local governments for 1965 are tied closely to the comparable figures for 1961, whereas earlier (see Table 3–5) we found that the 1961 figures were best predicted by the amount of state and local revenues per capita. The 1965 expenditures are also positively associated with the percentage of Vocational Act funds allocated to adult education, federal income and employment tax

[34] Grumm confirms this finding. "Structural Determinants of Legislative Output," p. 18.

[35] Sharkansky, *Spending in the American States,* p. 146.

Table 3–5 Correlations and Standardized Regression Coefficients for the Dependent Variable: Per Capita Educational Expenditures of State and Local Governments, 1961 (y)

Dependent Variable: Per capita educational expenditures of state and local governments, 1961: y_{73}

Independent Variable	Zero Order Correlation	Standardized Regression Coefficient
State and local revenues per capita, 1961: x_{82}	.869	.596
Median age of population, 1960: x_{21}	−.184	−.319
College enrollment per 10,000 population, 1964: x_{23}	.517	.286
Change in per capita income, 1950–60 (percentage of increase): x_{63}	−.496	−.170
Foreign and mixed parentage as a percentage of total population, 1960: x_{24}	.267	−.295
Median family income, 1959: x_{68}	.605	.227
Population per lawyer, 1963: x_{28}	−.235	.194
American Federation of Teachers membership, June 1966: x_{115}	.049	−.110
Federal percentage of total welfare expenditures, 1961: x_{98}	−.449	−.411
Party competition index for senate, 1963–64: x_{12}	.263	−.209
Percentage of Vocational Act funds allocated to adult education, 1965: x_{120}	−.185	−.160

R = .99*   Variance Explained = 97.5%

$$y^{**} = .2596x_{82} - .3201x_{21} + .1170x_{23} - .0488x_{63} - .0946x_{24} + .0061x_{68} + .0259x_{28}$$
$$\quad (.0279) \quad (.0740) \quad (.0205) \quad (.0139) \quad (.0223) \quad (.0019) \quad (.0084)$$
$$- .0500x_{115} - .0844x_{98} - .0229x_{12} - .0353x_{120} + 146.9301$$
$$\quad (.0245) \quad (.0224) \quad (.0069) \quad (.0110)$$

*Significant at the .001 level.

**Regression coefficients unstandardized; standard errors in parentheses.

Table 3-6 Correlations and Standardized Regression Coefficients for the Dependent Variable: Per Capita Educational Expenditures of State and Local Governments, 1965 (y)

Dependent Variable: Per capita educational expenditures of state and local governments, 1965: y_{127}

Independent Variable	Zero Order Correlation	Standardized Regression Coefficient
Per capita educational expenditures of state and local governments, 1961: x_{73}	.965	.845
Percentage of Vocational Act funds allocated to adult education, 1965: x_{120}	−.267	.034
Federal income and employment tax collections per capita, 1963: x_{40}	.355	.276
Number of telephones per 1,000 population, 1963: x_{29}	.273	−.397
Cultural enrichment, Hofferbert factor, 1960: x_{113}	.736	.458
State and local revenues per capita, 1961: x_{82}	.821	−.200

$$R = .98* \qquad \text{Variance Explained} = 96.9\%$$

$$y** = 1.1745x_{73} + .1004x_{120} + .0721x_{40} - .1878x_{29} + .0183x_{113} - .1213x_{82} + 108.2381$$
$$\quad (.1233) \qquad (.0155) \qquad (.0190) \qquad (.0492) \qquad (.0049) \qquad (.0579)$$

*Significant at the .001 level.

**Regression coefficients unstandardized; standard errors in parentheses.

collections per capita, and the "cultural enrichment" score developed by Hofferbert.[36] Independent variables that have negative effects are the number of telephones per 1,000 population and state and local revenues per capita.[37] Thus, the funds expended for education in a given state for a given time period appear to be more the product of federal government activity and the state's prior patterns of expenditures than the result of carefully balancing current needs against resources.

In Table 3–7 we find that the per capita educational expenditures of state and local governments for 1966 are similarly dependent upon those for the preceding period. The new variables positively associated with this dependent variable are the Gini index and the Negro percentage of total population, variables that inevitably focus our attention on the Southern states since those are the states showing the greatest inequality of income and the most racial heterogeneity. Surprisingly enough, disparities in income and racial makeup are positively correlated with per capita educational allocations by state and local governments, whereas the three political variables delineated are all negatively associated with educational expenditures.

Public School Expenditures per Pupil

Will public school expenditures consistently be associated with the same variables over time, or will variables important in the first time period be partialled out in subsequent time periods? Further, will social and political variables emerge as important secondary indicators? Upon examining public school expenditures per pupil, we find (much as expected) that they are most strongly related to economic variables. They are negatively associated with the number of legislators in a state and with the "index of malapportionment"

[36] Hofferbert, "Socioeconomic Dimensions of American States," pp. 408–9.

[37] We suggested earlier that primary predictor variables that are connected with a particular expenditure is an initial time period would likely be absorbed (controlled) in subsequent time periods. The appearance of state and local revenues per capita in a negative capacity is the first example of this phenomenon. Controlling in the stepwise regression program is done with the partial coefficient. Therefore, in this analysis partialling is analogous to controlling for a variable.

Table 3-7   Correlations and Standardized Regression Coefficients for the Dependent Variable: Per Capita Educational Expenditures of State and Local Governments, 1966 (y)

Dependent Variable: Per capita educational expenditures of state and local governments, 1966: y_{128}

Independent Variable	Zero Order Correlation	Standardized Regression Coefficient
Per capita educational expenditures of state and local governments, 1965: x_{127}	.969	.980
Gini index, 1959: x_{111}	−.028	.196
Percentage of membership in senate from majority party, 1954–62: x_{69}	−.457	−.397
Party competition index for senate, 1963–64: x_{12}	.257	−.290
Negro percentage of population, 1960: x_{20}	−.526	.370
Average winning percentage in gubernatorial elections, 1954–62: x_{70}	−.485	−.265

R = .99*   Variance Explained = 98.6%

$$y** = 1.0818x_{127} + .0296x_{111} - .9842x_{69} - .0487x_{12} + .1460x_{20} - .0820x_{70} + 135.8887$$
$$(.0359) \quad\quad (.0049) \quad\quad (.1662) \quad\quad (.0087) \quad\quad (.0285) \quad\quad (.0198)$$

*Significant at the .001 level.

**Regression coefficients unstandardized; standard errors in parentheses.

developed by Manning J. Dauer and Robert G. Kelsay,[38] leading us to believe that political variables in general may be negatively related to this dependent variable.

In examining public school expenditures per pupil in 1963 (see Table 3–8), we find that median family income, state and local taxes per capita, and the median age of a state's residents are all positively associated with this variable for both the zero order correlation and the standardized regression coefficients. Interestingly, once state and local taxes and changes in income are accounted for, the estimated market value of property per capita moves from a positive to a negative correlation; similarly, the political and welfare variables that appear are negatively associated with the dependent variable.

Does this pattern recur consistently? When this dependent variable is considered over time (see Tables 3–9 and 3–10), the previous year's expenditures become most influential in determining current expenditures. In addition, in the figures for 1965, retail sales per capita change from a positive zero order correlation to a strong negative regression coefficient, a reversal confirmed in the Zeigler-Johnson study of educational innovation.[39] We would expect that in central cities where retail sales per capita are strongly related to educational allocations, retail merchants will continue to be predisposed against educational expenditures. In the suburbs the relationship between retail sales and educational expenditures will probably remain positive if only because the merchants and retail employees will demand and support superior educational facilities for their own children. The course of suburbanization, we assume, continues to be a factor related to per pupil expenditures in the public schools. These conclusions remain to be tested, however, within future studies.

As a general rule, one-way political variables are negatively related to public school expenditures per pupil when other variables are controlled. Controlling for the other variables, we find in Table 3–9 that a high urban population percentage and a high proportion of

[38] This index is available in Paul T. David and Ralph Eisenberg, *Devaluation of the Urban and Suburban Vote* (Charlottesville, Va.: Bureau of Public Administration, University of Virginia, 1961), p. 5.
[39] Zeigler and Johnson, "Educational Innovation and Politico-Economic Systems," pp. 161–76.

Table 3-8 Correlations and Standardized Regression Coefficients for the Dependent Variable: Public School Expenditures Per Pupil, 1963

Dependent Variable: Public school expenditures per pupil, 1963: y_{48}

Independent Variable	Zero Order Correlation	Standardized Regression Coefficient
Median family income, 1959: x_{68}	.848	.376
State and local taxes per capita, 1963: x_{41}	.847	.433
Change in per capita income, 1950–60: x_{63}	−.592	−.273
Estimated market value of property per capita, 1961: x_{31}	.456	−.243
Median age of population, 1960: x_{21}	.450	.365
Voter turnout in gubernatorial and senatorial elections in non-Presidential election years, 1952–60: x_{57}	.511	−.195
Per capita educational expenditures of state and local governments, 1961: x_{73}	.608	.246
General assistance cases as a percentage of total population: x_{99}	.434	−.112

$R = .95^{*}$ Variance Explained = 90.2%

$$y^{**} = .0355x_{68} + .9210x_{41} - .2779x_{63} - .0182x_{31} + 1.2998x_{21} - .1058x_{57} + .8727x_{73}$$
$$(.0122) \quad (.3667) \quad (.0929) \quad (.0072) \quad (.4481) \quad (.0547) \quad (.5423)$$
$$- .0810x_{99} - 161.9244$$
$$(.0639)$$

*Significant at the .001 level.

**Regression coefficients unstandardized; standard errors in parentheses.

Table 3-9   Correlations and Standardized Regression Coefficients for the Dependent Variable:
Public School Expenditures Per Pupil, 1964

Dependent Variable: Public school expenditures per pupil, 1964: y_{125}

Independent Variable	Zero Order Correlation	Standardized Regression Coefficient
Public school expenditures per pupil, 1963: x_{48}	.976	.893
State and local taxes per capita, 1963: x_{41}	.852	.107
Aid to the blind, average monthly payment per recipient, December 1964: x_{53}	.549	.038
Urban population, percentage of population residing in state's largest SMSA, 1963: x_{25}	.435	−.076
Paroled prisoners as a percentage of all releases, 1960: x_{110}	.364	−.032
American Federation of Teachers membership, June 1966: x_{115}	.294	.155
Draft board mental test, percentage of failures, 1963: x_{27}	−.582	.258
Democratic percentage of membership in lower house, 1963: x_{95}	.519	−.203
Median school years completed by persons over twenty-five, 1960: x_{22}	.625	.049
Population per lawyer, 1963: x_{28}	−.604	−.159
Number of telephones per 1,000 population, 1963: x_{29}	.627	−.172
Old age assistance, average monthly payment per recipient, December 1964: x_{51}	.576	−.117
Cultural enrichment, Hofferbert factor, 1960: x_{113}	.661	.126

R = .99*   Variance Explained = 97.4%

$$
\begin{aligned}
y^{**} = {} & 1.0141x_{48} + .2594x_{41} + .1975x_{53} - .0449x_{25} - .1036x_{110} + .2830x_{115} + .2113x_{27} \\
& \;(.0991) \quad (.2887) \quad (.4703) \quad (.0481) \quad (.0225) \quad (.1419) \quad (.0939) \\
& - .0926x_{95} + .4838x_{22} + .0856x_{28} - .2361x_{29} - .8067x_{51} + .0146x_{113} + 162.7400 \\
& \;(.0445) \quad (1.1013) \quad (.0439) \quad (.1478) \quad (.6470) \quad (.0148)
\end{aligned}
$$

*Significant at the .001 level.

**Regression coefficient unstandardized; standard errors in parentheses.

Table 3–10 Correlations and Standardized Regression Coefficients for the Dependent Variable: Public School Expenditures Per Pupil, 1965 (y)

Dependent Variable: Public school expenditures per pupil, 1965: y_{126}

Independent Variable	Zero Order Correlation	Standardized Regression Coefficient
Public school expenditures per pupil, 1964: x_{125}	.964	.797
Retail sales per capita, 1963: x_{36}	.510	−.424
Public school expenditures per pupil, 1963: x_{48}	.960	.450
Per capita state expenditure for correctional system, 1961: x_{85}	.578	−.136
Cultural enrichment, Hofferbert factor, 1960: x_{113}	.580	.387
State and local revenues per capita, 1961: x_{82}	.650	−.167
Party competition index for lower house, 1963–64: x_{13}	.529	−.095

R = .99*   Variance Explained = 97.1%

$$y^{**} = .7838x_{125} - 2.5149x_{36} + .5024x_{48} - .1198x_{85} + .0441x_{113} - .2885x_{82} - .0362x_{13}$$
$$(.1820) \quad (.6480) \quad (.2035) \quad (.0497) \quad (.0165) \quad (.1497) \quad (.0199)$$
$$+ 393.2470$$

*Significant at the .001 level.

**Regression coefficients unstandardized; standard errors in parentheses.

Democrats in the lower house are both negatively related to educational expenditures. We would expect, though, that assistance to the blind, the aged, and the infirm might indicate a state's relative willingness to spend money for education.

Do these same variables emerge when we deliberately exclude the previous year's expenditures from our regression analysis? In examining public school expenditures per pupil for 1964 independently of the 1963 figures (see Table 3–11), we find that taxation and income variables are still most strongly related to the dependent variable. Since educational expenditures per pupil are related to wide-ranging economic and social variables, we might expect the percentage of school revenues contributed by the state to be related to these same variables; in other words, we might expect that the economic variables influential in determining the level of per pupil expenditure would also help to determine the proportion of the educational burden assumed by the state.

Percentage of School Revenues from State

The expected close relationship between this dependent variable and economic variables simply does not materialize. In Tables 3–12 and 3–13 we see that the political variables are all positively related to the state's share of educational outlays with but one exception, namely, the Democratic percentage of membership in the state senate. Contrary to our expectations, we find that for (fiscal) 1964 the independent variable related most positively to our dependent variable is the Democratic percentage of the two-party membership in the lower house. Much as expected, the party competition index for the senate correlates positively with a high percentage of educational expenditures derived from the state. General assistance cases as a percentage of the total population show a slightly positive correlation in the standardized regression coefficient, but the two other welfare variables, aid to the blind and old age assistance, show negative correlations. We conclude tentatively that political variables are key determinants of the proportion of state contributions to education.

If the foregoing conclusion is correct, James B. Conant's plan for educational finance wherein states would have complete control over the disbursement of federal educational grants would probably

Table 3–11 Correlations and Standardized Regression Coefficients for the Dependent Variable: Public School Expenditures Per Pupil, 1964 (y), Without 1963 Expenditures (x_{48})

Dependent Variable: Public school expenditures per pupil, 1964: y_{125}

Independent Variable	Zero Order Correlation	Standardized Regression Coefficient
State and local taxes per capita, 1963: x_{41}	.852	.645
Median family income, 1959: x_{68}	.827	.289
Change in per capita income, 1950–60: x_{63}	−.571	−.161
Estimated market value of property per capita, 1961: x_{31}	.449	−.284
Population per lawyer, 1963: x_{28}	−.604	−.303
College enrollment per 10,000 population, 1964: x_{23}	.291	−.158
Percentage of Vocational Act funds allocated to adult education, 1965: x_{120}	−.251	−.089
Percentage of membership in senate from majority party, 1954–62: x_{69}	−.608	.094
Paroled prisoners as a percentage of all releases: x_{110}	.364	.112
Gini index: x_{111}	−.457	.129
Number of telephones per 1,000 population, 1963: x_{29}	.627	−.350
Median age of population, 1960: x_{21}	.442	.266
Per capita federal grants to state and local governments for health, welfare, and related activities, 1961: x_{81}	−.369	−.149
Per capita educational expenditures of state and local governments, 1961: x_{73}	.602	.205

Table 3-11 (continued)

$$R = .96^*$$

Variance Explained = 91.3%

$$y^{**} = 1.5586x_{41} + .0310x_{68} - .1854x_{63} - .0242x_{31} - .1631x_{28} - .2601x_{23} - .0789x_{120}$$
$$\quad (.5471) \quad (.0199) \quad (.1494) \quad (.0103) \quad (.0822) \quad (.2035) \quad (.1016)$$
$$\quad + .6090x_{69} + .0481x_{110} + .0515x_{111} - .4795x_{29} + 1.0760x_{21} - .2149x_{81} + .8260x_{73}$$
$$\quad (.9780) \quad (.0503) \quad (.0509) \quad (.3217) \quad (.7199) \quad (.1827) \quad (.8797)$$
$$\quad + 113.4911$$

*Significant at the .001 level.

**Regression coefficients unstandardized; standard errors in parentheses.

Table 3-12 Correlations and Standardized Regression Coefficients for the Dependent Variable: Percentage of School Revenues from State, 1964

Dependent Variable: Percentage of school revenues from state, 1964: y_{135}

Independent Variable	Zero Order Correlation	Standardized Regression Coefficient
Democratic percentage of two-party membership in lower house, 1963–64: x_{16}	.705	.801
Old age assistance, average monthly payment per recipient, December 1964: x_{51}	−.593	−.613
Per capita state expenditures for correctional system, 1961: x_{85}	.031	.375
Percentage of Vocational Act funds allocated to adult education, 1965: x_{120}	.359	.297
Party competition index for senate, 1963–64: x_{12}	−.052	.557
Gini index, 1959: x_{111}	.438	.318
Democratic percentage of membership in senate, 1963: x_{96}	.626	−.593
General assistance cases as percentage of total population, 1961: x_{99}	−.175	.296
Percentage of membership in senate from majority party, 1954–62: x_{69}	.372	.540
Educational innovation, 1966: x_{124}	.093	.185

$$R = .98* \qquad \text{Variance Explained} = 95.2\%$$

$$
\begin{aligned}
y^{**} = \; & .5376x_{16} - 7.9672x_{51} + .6344x_{85} + .4990x_{120} + .4630x_{12} + .2386x_{111} - .4678x_{96} \\
& (.0577) \quad (1.0368) \quad\;\; (.1194) \quad\;\; (.1050) \quad\;\; (.0731) \quad\;\; (.0539) \quad\;\;\; (.0939) \\
& + .4594x_{99} + 6.6353x_{69} + 2.8140x_{124} - 312.7189 \\
& \;\;\;(.1051) \quad\;\; (1.5255) \quad\;\; (1.1085)
\end{aligned}
$$

*Significant at the .001 level.

**Regression coefficients unstandardized; standard errors in parentheses.

Table 3–13 Correlations and Standardized Regression Coefficients for the Dependent Variable: Percentage of School Revenues from State, 1965 (y)

Dependent Variable: Percentage of school revenues from state, 1965: y_{136}

Independent Variable	Zero Order Correlation	Standardized Regression Coefficient
Percentage of school revenues from state, 1964: x_{135}	+.978	.897
General assistance cases as a percentage of total population: x_{99}	−.098	.107
Aid to the blind, average monthly payment per recipient, December 1964: x_{53}	−.331	−.110
Percentage of Vocational Act funds allocated to adult education, 1965: x_{120}	.417	.153
Party competition index for senate, 1963–64: x_{12}	−.052	.294
Percentage of membership in senate from majority party, 1954–62: x_{69}	.360	.301
Negro percentage of population, 1960, x_{20}	.520	−.165

R = .99*   Variance Explained = 99.0%

$$y^{**} = .7357x_{135} + .1367x_{89} - .8815x_{53} + .2108x_{120} + .2004x_{12} + 3.0344x_{69} - .2641x_{20}$$
$$\phantom{y^{**} =}\ (.0234)\quad (.0338)\quad (.2246)\quad (.0419)\quad (.0330)\quad (.6333)\quad (.0730)$$
$$- 207.1258$$

*Significant at the .001 level.

**Regression coefficients unstandardized; standard errors in parentheses.

only intensify the political problems already existing at the state level.[40] Also, as localities begin to obtain greater control of their educational funding, we can expect to see a new wave of intergovernmental conflicts developing between cities and states.

In contrast to the findings of Ira Sharkansky and Wayne L. Francis, Thomas R. Dye has found that the state's share of educational outlays is strongly related to Democratic control of the legislative houses and the governor's chair.[41] We would merely add that this dependent variable is positively associated with the party competition index for the various state senates. Our conclusion remains that the percentage of school revenues derived from the state is primarily the product of prior allocations and political determinants.

Educational Innovation

Within our progressive liberalism factor, we find that an interesting pattern emerges for educational innovation (see Table 3–14). Per capita income, the number of telephones per 1,000 population, and urban population are the most important variables related to educational innovation in the zero order correlations. When we control for the other variables, however, a different ordering of items emerges. In examining the standardized regression coefficients, we find that the Democratic percentage of the two-party vote for President, the party competition index for the lower house, the average percentage of Democratic votes for governor, and the number of telephones per 1,000 population (a measure of urbanization) emerge as better variables for explaining high educational innovation than per capita income.

The positive correlations for per capita income and urban population are consistent with previous findings and emerge first in the unstandardized regression analysis, indicating that under present circumstances and given unequal contributions of economic, social, and political variables, educational innovation will be affected most dramatically by income levels. Whenever all the variables are put on

[40] See Calvin Grieder, "New Conant Plan Raises Some Searching Questions," *Nations Schools* 82 (November 1968): 6; and "Conant State Finance Plan Gets Qualified Approval," *Nations Schools* 83 (January 1969): 70–71.

[41] Dye, *Politics, Economics, and the Public*, pp. 258–67.

Table 3–14 Correlations and Standardized Regression Coefficients for the Dependent Variable: Educational Innovation, 1966 (y)

Dependent Variable: Educational innovation, 1966: y_{124}

Independent Variable	Zero Order Correlation	Standardized Regression Coefficient
Per capita income, 1963: x_{32}	.693	.314
Urban population, percentage of population residing in state's largest SMSA, 1963: x_{25}	.590	.048
Change in percentage of Negro population, 1950–63: x_{67}	.298	−.659
Democratic percentage of two-party vote for President, 1964: x_{58}	.538	.805
Federal percentage of total welfare expenditures, 1961: x_{98}	−.582	.249
Average Democratic percentage in gubernatorial elections, 1956–62: x_{97}	−.150	.638
Party competition index for lower house, 1963–64: x_{13}	.275	.766
Number of telephones per 1,000 population, 1963: x_{29}	.607	.600

$$R = .90^* \qquad \text{Variance Explained} = 81.6\%$$

$$y^{**} = .0091x_{32} + .0035x_{25} - .6278x_{67} + .1031x_{58} + .0256x_{98} + .0643x_{97} + .0368x_{13}$$
$$\quad\ \ (.0056) \quad (.0097) \quad (.1823) \quad (.0235) \quad (.0285) \quad (.0184) \quad (.0120)$$
$$+ .1020x_{29} + 490.3647$$
$$\ \ (.0452)$$

*Significant at the .001 level.

**Regression coefficients unstandardized; standard errors in parentheses.

an equal footing, however, political variables will be most influential in the adoption of educational innovations. We might further infer from the findings that once income and urbanization are controlled, areas that have experienced a large influx of Negroes would likely suffer the greatest in trying to institute educational innovations. Our general conclusion is that as more federal funds become available, as the interplay of partisan competition increases, as the Democratic party (particularly in the South) becomes more flexible, and as urbanization and welfare spending become set patterns of life, the adoption of educational innovations will become more widespread. Certainly this conclusion has important implications. Urban school districts that are wealthy, characterized by intense partisan competition, and interested in obtaining grants from federal and state agencies will continue to experiment most in educational innovation. Similarly, wealthy industrialized states that attempt to obtain their full share of federal funds and that are characterized by intense partisan competition will likely support and encourage greater educational innovation.

Percentage of Vocational Act Funds Allocated to Adult Education

In Table 3–15 we find that the average winning percentage in gubernatorial elections for the period 1954–62, while strongly correlated with the percentage of Vocational Act funds allocated to adult education in 1965, becomes even more strongly correlated when we standardize the measure. Similarly, general assistance, a slightly negative correlate at the zero order level, becomes a strong positive indicator of allocations for adult education whenever we impose statistical controls. The Gini index, a measure of the degree of income inequality within a state, reflects the economic and political realities implied in distributions for adult education. We would expect that the Southern states, which have high gubernatorial majorities as well as great disparities in the distribution of income within their borders, will direct a disproportionate share of Vocational Act funds into adult education projects.

Thus, a political variable reflecting the lack of partisan competition within a state, a welfare variable indicating unsatisfied needs among a state's residents, and an economic variable reflecting great

Table 3–15 Correlations and Standardized Regression Coefficients for the Dependent Variable: Percentage of Vocational Act Funds Allocated to Adult Education, 1965 (y)

Dependent Variable: Percentage of Vocational Act funds allocated to adult education, 1965: y_{120}

Independent Variable	Zero Order Correlation	Standardized Regression Coefficient
Average winning percentage in gubernatorial elections, 1954-62: x_{70}	.625	.761
General assistance, average monthly payment per case, December 1961: x_{74}	−.057	.446
Gini index, 1959: x_{111}	.351	.225

$$R = .73^*$$

$$y^{**} = \underset{(.0674)}{.6944x_{70}} + \underset{(.3609)}{2.2591x_{74}} + \underset{(.0242)}{.1006x_{111}} - 505.0121$$

Variance Explained = 52.9%

*Significant at the .001 level.

**Regression coefficients unstandardized; standard errors in parentheses.

disparities in income among the residents combine to explain the disproportionate emphasis on adult education programs in Southern states' disbursement of Vocational Act funds. Most Southern governors (Terry Sanford of North Carolina being a notable exception) have tended to direct Vocational Act funds to programs that have reinforced segregationist policies. Adult education and construction programs represent a relatively safe way of keeping federal funds out of civil rights controversies. Thus we see that just as the state's share of educational outlays reflects political attitudes, so likewise does the state's distribution of federal funds to adult education.

Will political variables continue to emerge as strong predictors of educational policy outcomes? Thus far our analysis has suggested that, all other things being equal, economic outcomes (i.e., expenditures) are most closely associated with economic variables while noneconomic outcomes are most closely associated with political variables.

American Federation of Teachers Membership

In Table 3–16 we find that the most important variable related to American Federation of Teachers membership is, as expected, urban population—specifically, the percentage of the population living in the state's largest standard metropolitan statistical area (SMSA)— followed by foreign and mixed parentage as a percentage of the total population. Party competition in the senate and two welfare variables are also positively associated with AFT membership. Surprisingly, the amount of federal income and employment tax collections per capita is negatively associated with the dependent variable, as are likewise party competition in the lower house, aid to the disabled, and two economic variables.

While a definite pattern of membership proclivities is evident among the various states, we might speculate that as the National Education Association becomes increasingly conscious of the rising tide of teacher militancy that organization might begin to co-opt the tactics and positions of the American Federation of Teachers. If the NEA fails to reflect the prevailing values of urban teachers, its membership figures will doubtless suffer.

As Table 3–17 amply indicates, the variables most closely associ-

Table 3–16 Correlations and Standardized Regression Coefficients for the Dependent Variable: American Federation of Teachers Membership, June 1966 (y)

Dependent Variable: American Federation of Teachers membership, June 1966: y_{115}

Independent Variable	Zero Order Correlation	Standardized Regression Coefficient
Urban population, percentage of population living in the state's largest SMSA, 1963: x_{25}	.679	.939
Foreign and mixed parentage as a percentage of total population, 1960: x_{24}	.564	.295
Federal income and employment tax collections per capita, 1963: x_{40}	.315	−.712
Party competition index for senate, 1963–64: x_{12}	.425	.664
General assistance cases as a percentage of total population, 1961: x_{99}	.431	.350
Party competition index for lower house, 1963–64: x_{13}	.233	−.448
State and local tax revenues per capita, 1961: x_{83}	.326	−.533
Aid to the disabled, recipients per 100,000 population, December 1961: x_{108}	−.261	−.373
Change in per capita income, 1950–60 (percentage of increase): x_{63}	−.280	−.264
Old age assistance, average monthly payment per recipient, December 1964: x_{51}	.332	.316
Average Democratic percentage in gubernatorial elections, 1956–62: x_{97}	−.245	.296

$$R = .98^* \qquad \text{Variance Explained} = 95.6\%$$

$$
\begin{aligned}
y^{**} = \ & .3032x_{25} + .2084x_{24} - 1.3881x_{108} - .2952x_{40} + .1603x_{12} + .1575x_{99} - .0951x_{13} \\
& (.0278) \quad (.0614) \quad\ (.3085) \qquad (.0379) \quad\ (.0189) \quad\ (.0315) \quad\ (.0190) \\
& - .1670x_{63} + 1.1911x_{51} + .1319x_{97} - .7473x_{83} + 59.1491 \\
& \ \ (.0413) \qquad (.3096) \quad\ (.0382) \quad\ (.1381)
\end{aligned}
$$

*Significant at the .001 level.

**Regression coefficients unstandardized; standard errors in parentheses.

Table 3-17 Correlations and Standardized Regression Coefficients for the Dependent Variable: National Education Association Membership, June 1966

Dependent Variable: National Education Association membership, June 1966: y_{114}

Independent Variable	*Zero Order Correlation*	*Standardized Regression Coefficient*
Foreign and mixed parentage as a percentage of total population, 1960: x_{24}	−.292	−.317
Party competition index for lower house, 1963–64: x_{13}	.035	.407
Federal income and employment tax collections per capita, 1963: x_{40}	−.262	−.134
General assistance cases as a percentage of total population, 1961: x_{99}	−.141	−.154
Party competition index for senate, 1963–64: x_{12}	−.138	−.160

$$R = .43* \qquad \text{Variance Explained} = 18.5\%$$

$$y** = -.0823x_{24} + .0318x_{13} - .0205x_{40} - .0255x_{99} - .0142x_{12} + 71.363$$
$$ (.0503) \quad (.0192) \quad (.0327) \quad (.0348) \quad (.0205)$$

*Not significant.

**Regression coefficients unstandardized; standard errors in parentheses.

ated with AFT membership are unimportant in predicting NEA membership. For example, NEA membership is negatively related to the percentage of persons of foreign or mixed parentage and to party competition in the senate, two variables that were positively related to AFT membership. Conversely, it is positively related to party competition in the lower house, a variable negatively associated with AFT membership. Moreover, these five variables together explain less than one-fifth of the total variance in the dependent variable.

If the American Federation of Teachers continues to concentrate its recruitment efforts in urban industrialized areas, and if simultaneously the National Education Association begins to adopt tactics and positions heretofore identified with the AFT, we may expect increasing rivalry and some measure of confrontation between the two groups.

In examining the last three dependent variables, we turn our attention from the progressive liberalism factor to the federalism-and-concern factor.

Per Capita Expenditures for Higher Education

For fiscal 1964 the variable related most positively to per capita expenditures for higher education is general innovation, whereas the number of students per classroom is a negative indicator (see Table 3–18). Over time, our analysis shows that per capita expenditures for higher education in 1964 explain about 80 percent of the variance in the comparable expenditures for fiscal 1966 (see Table 3–19). Among the other positive variables, only the percentage of state and local revenues from the federal government is substantially related to the dependent variable. The other positive variables of lesser importance are per capita state expenditures for its correctional system and the percentage of Vocational Act funds allocated to postsecondary education, whereas the federal percentage of total educational expenditures and federal grants to state and local governments per capita are both relatively unimportant negative correlates.

Percentage of Vocational Act Funds Allocated to Postsecondary Education

Economic variables alone do not significantly explain the percentage of Vocational Act funds allocated to postsecondary education.

Table 3-18 Correlations and Standardized Regression Coefficients for the Dependent Variable: Per Capita Expenditures for Higher Education, 1964 (y)

Dependent Variable: Per capita expenditures for higher education, 1964: y_{143}

Independent Variable	Zero Order Correlation	Standardized Regression Coefficient
General innovation: x_{123}	.518	.574
Number of students per classroom, 1964: x_{50}	−.204	−.308

$$R = .60^* \qquad \text{Variance Explained} = 36.0\%$$

$$y^{**} = .1002x_{123} - .1863x_{50} + 48.6316$$
$$\quad\;\; (.0233) \qquad (.0808)$$

*Significant at the .01 level.

**Regression coefficients unstandardized; standard errors in parentheses.

Table 3–19 Correlations and Standardized Regression Coefficients for the Dependent Variable: Per Capita Expenditures for Higher Education, 1966 (y)

Dependent Variable: Per capita expenditures for higher education, 1966: y_{144}

Independent Variable	Zero Order Correlation	Standardized Regression Coefficient
Per capita expenditures for higher education, 1964: x_{143}	.929	.895
Percentage of Vocational Act funds allocated to higher education, 1965: x_{119}	.003	.103
Percentage of state and local revenues from federal government, 1963: x_{43}	−.014	.312
Federal percentage of total educational expenditures, 1961: x_{72}	−.142	−.144
Per capita state expenditures for correctional system, 1961: x_{85}	.443	.129
Federal grants to state and local governments per capita, 1963: x_{39}	.074	−.178

$R = .94*$ Variance Explained = 89.3%

$$y** = 1.1775x_{143} + .0101x_{119} + .1052x_{43} - .0722x_{72} + .0211x_{85} - .1315x_{39} - 6.5756$$
$$\quad\;\; (.0870) \qquad (.0069) \qquad (.0513) \qquad (.0435) \qquad (.0124) \qquad (.1111)$$

*Significant at the .001 level.

**Regression coefficients unstandardized; standard errors in parentheses.

Whereas the variables in the federalism-and-concern factor explained almost 90 percent of the variance in per capita expenditures for higher education, they are able to explain only about 30 percent of the variation in this dependent variable (see Table 3–20).

Within each state the legislature decides how Vocational Act funds will be distributed. Although the law requires that one-third of the funds be devoted to construction or to postsecondary vocational education, the legislatures do not always comply with this regulation (Delaware, for example, once funneled 100 percent of its Vocational Act funds into secondary school programs). In Table 3–20 we find that the two variables most closely associated with our dependent variable are state and local expenditures for welfare as a percentage of personal income and the change in value added by agriculture for the period 1950–60. The pattern appears to be that as more funds become available, postsecondary vocational education allocations tend to follow the direction of general welfare expenditures in the state. That is, as the percentage of state and local funds allocated to welfare increases, we would expect the distribution of Vocational Act funds to be increasingly weighted in favor of postsecondary education. The importance of agriculture within a state has considerable relevance to that state's vocational education program; as agricultural technology becomes more refined through the development of new machinery and farming techniques, training is needed to enable farm managers and workers to understand these new methods and devices. Even though they may not emphasize adult education goals, the extension programs for post–high school education tend to increase in states where modern farming techniques are widely accepted and put into practice.

Number of Students per Classroom

Of our nine dependent variables, the one least amenable to analysis is the number of students per classroom. For 1964 (see Table 3–21), the variance explained for this variable is only 16 percent, accounted for by the Democratic percentage of two-party membership in the state senate during the 1963–64 biennium. Once the number of students per classroom is established for 1964, the pattern for subsequent years becomes dominated by the previous

Table 3-20 Correlations and Standardized Regression Coefficients for the Dependent Variable: Percentage of Vocational Act Funds Allocated to Postsecondary Education, 1965 (y)

Dependent Variable: Percentage of Vocational Act funds allocated to postsecondary education, 1965: y_{119}		
Independent Variable	Zero Order Correlation	Standardized Regression Coefficient
State and local expenditures for welfare as a percentage of personal income, 1961: x_{86}	.488	.476
Change in value added by agriculture, 1950–60: x_{64}	.262	.238

$$R = .54^*\qquad \text{Variance Explained} = 29.5\%$$

$$y^{**} = 6.5115 x_{86} + 2.1797 x_{64} - 200.8295$$
$$\phantom{y^{**} = }(1.8907)\quad\ (1.2682)$$

*Significant at the .01 level.
**Regression coefficients unstandardized; standard errors in parentheses.

Table 3-21 Correlations and Standardized Regression Coefficients for the Dependent Variable: Number of Students Per Classroom, 1964 (y)

Dependent Variable: Number of students per classroom, 1964: y_{50}

Independent Variable	Zero Order Correlation	Standardized Regression Coefficient
Democratic percentage of two-party membership in senate, 1963–64: x_{15}	.402	.402

$$R = .402^* \quad\quad \text{Variance Explained} = 16.1\%$$

$$y^{**} = .0096x_{15} + 252.9360$$
$$\quad\quad (.0036)$$

*Significant at the .05 level.

**Regression coefficients unstandardized; standard errors in parentheses.

year's reading. Thus, for 1965 (see Table 3–22) the number of students per classroom is most highly correlated with the comparable figure for 1964 (85.7 percent of variance explained). Similarly, the figures for 1965 constitute the dominant explanatory variable for the number of students per classroom in 1966 (see Table 3–23), although in this case other independent variables become relevant to the dependent variable.

Interestingly enough, per capita expenditures on the legislative branch are negatively associated with high student-classroom ratios, whereas the per capita expenditures on the compensation of the legislators are positively associated with these ratios. Thus we may detect the following pattern: small student-classroom ratios are most apt to be found in states that spend relatively large amounts of money on running the legislature but relatively little on legislators' salaries. In a way, this pattern seems reasonable. In thinking about student-classroom ratios, one should understand that large numbers of students per classroom are associated with either a state's inability (through lack of resources) or its unwillingness to expend sufficient funds to prevent overcrowding. Thus, legislators that would be willing to spend large amounts of money for staff, facilities, and legislative services would be correspondingly likely to spend the taxpayers' money to relieve overcrowding in classrooms. Similarly, legislators that would be willing to spend disproportionately large sums on their own salaries irrespective of the state's fiscal position might well be expected to put up with high levels of crowding in the state's classrooms. Not surprisingly, we find that the relationship between educational expenditures and student-classroom ratios is negative.

Changes in State Educational Expenditures

To this point we have been pursuing two main lines of development: first, we have been seeking to identify economic and noneconomic variables that explain educational outcomes, and second, we have been attempting to show that prior allocations are an important variable in predicting educational policy outcomes. We have accomplished neither of these tasks completely to our satisfaction, however. Next, let us consider to what extent prior allocations help to explain changes in educational allocations from one time period to another.

Table 3-22 Correlations and Standardized Regression Coefficients for the Dependent Variable: Number of Students Per Classroom, 1965 (y)

Dependent Variable: Number of students per classroom, 1965: y_{145}

Independent Variable	Zero Order Correlation	Standardized Regression Coefficient
Number of students per classroom, 1964: x_{50}	.926	.926

$$\mathbf{R} = .926* \qquad \text{Variance Explained} = 85.7\%$$

$$y** = .0088x_{50} + .2799$$
$$\quad\;\;(.0006)$$

*Significant at the .001 level.

**Regression coefficients unstandardized; standard errors in parentheses.

Table 3–23 Correlations and Standardized Regression Coefficients for the Dependent Variable: Number of Students Per Classroom, 1966

Dependent Variable: Number of students per classroom, 1966: y_{146} (y)

Independent Variable	*Zero Order Correlation*	*Standardized Regression Coefficient*
Number of students per classroom, 1965: x_{145}	.745	.817
Per capita expenditures on the legislative branch, 1963–64 biennium: x_8	−.321	−.575
Per capita state expenditures for correctional system, 1961: x_{85}	−.061	.114
Per capita expenditures on compensation of legislators, 1963–64 biennium: x_{10}	−.201	.319
Democratic percentage of two-party membership in senate, 1963–64: x_{15}	−.020	−.166

R = .85*   Variance Explained = 72.6%

$$y^{**} = .9633x_{145} - .0016x_8 + .0003x_{85} + .0020x_{10} - .0000x_{15} + .0714$$
$$\quad\quad (.1155) \quad\quad (.0004) \quad\quad (.0002) \quad\quad (.0013) \quad\quad (.0000)$$

*Significant at the .001 level.

**Regression coefficients unstandardized; standard errors in parentheses.

Instead of examining each of the nine dependent variables discussed earlier, we shall use only three: public school expenditures per pupil (a variable best defined by economic variables and prior allocations); the percentage of school revenues derived from the state (best defined by political variables and by prior allocations); and per capita expenditures for higher education (best defined by welfare and economic variables, as well as by prior allocations). Concentrating on the changes in these dependent variables, we will test two additional hypotheses:

PROPOSITION 10: *Changes in educational expenditures will be explained best by immediate prior allocations.*

PROPOSITION 11: *With respect to changes in educational expenditures over more than one time period, current changes will be most closely associated with changes in the earlier time period.*

Proposition 10 constitutes a starting point for the study of change whereas Proposition 11 says something about the relationship between one change and another.[42]

From fiscal 1963 to fiscal 1964 (see Table 3–24) the change in public school expenditures per pupil is best defined by an economic variable, namely, state and local taxes per capita. Interestingly enough, when welfare benefits (specifically, payments to the blind) increase, public school expenditures tend to decline. Changes in per pupil expenditures do not, however, appear to be strongly related to prior allocations ($r = .160$ for 1963).

From 1964 to 1965 (see Table 3–25) the change in public school expenditures per pupil increases most positively with prior expenditures at the standardized regression level. Surprisingly, retail sales per capita, an economic variable, is at both levels the strongest negative correlate.

For the change in the percentage of school revenues derived from the state from fiscal 1962 to fiscal 1964 (see Table 3–26), we find that the allocations for 1962 appear nowhere in the regression equation. The correlation between the 1962 figures and the dependent

---

[42] The predictive aspect of linear regression is really the main thrust of our analysis; see Elliot R. Morss, "Some Thoughts on the Determinants of State and Local Expenditures," *National Tax Journal* 19 (March 1966): 99.

Table 3–24   Correlations and Standardized Regression Coefficients for the Dependent Variable: Change in Public School Expenditures Per Pupil, 1963 to 1964

Dependent Variable: Change in public school expenditures per pupil, 1963 to 1964 (y)

Independent Variable	Zero Order Correlation	Standardized Regression Coefficient
State and local taxes per capita, 1963: x_{41}	.444	.639
Aid to the blind, average monthly payment per recipient, December 1964: x_{53}	.190	−.270

$$R = .48^* \qquad \text{Variance Explained} = 23.2\%$$

$$y^{**} = \underset{(.106)}{.369x_{41}} - \underset{(.227)}{.333x_{53}} - 3.905$$

*Not significant.

**Regression coefficients unstandardized; standard errors in parentheses.

Table 3–25 Correlations and Standardized Regression Coefficients for the Dependent Variable: Change in Public School Expenditures Per Pupil, 1964 to 1965 (y)

Dependent Variable: Change in public school expenditures per pupil, 1964 to 1965 (y)

Independent Variable	Zero Order Correlation	Standardized Regression Coefficient
Retail sales per capita, 1963: x_{36}	−.497	−.802
Public school expenditures per pupil, 1963: x_{48}	−.119	1.399
Public school expenditures per pupil, 1964: x_{125}	−.193	.916
Democratic percentage of two-party membership in lower house, 1963–64: x_{16}	.420	.400
Per capita state expenditures for correctional system, 1961: x_{85}	−.239	−.372
Draft board mental test, percentage of failures, 1963: x_{27}	.252	−.478
General assistance, average payment per case, December 1961: x_{74}	−.233	−.283
Federal income and employment tax collections per capita, 1963: x_{40}	−.101	.269

$$R = .76^* \qquad \text{Variance Explained} = 58.3\%$$

$$y^{**} = -1.286x_{36} + .423x_{48} - .244x_{125} + .036x_{16} - .089x_{85} - .104x_{27} - .340x_{74}$$
$$\phantom{y^{**} =}(.273)\quad(.153)\quad(.128)\quad(-.125)\quad(.032)\quad(.041)\quad(.174)$$
$$- .051x_{40} + 172.781$$
$$\phantom{y^{**} =}(.030)$$

*Significant at the .05 level.
**Regression coefficients unstandardized; standard errors in parentheses.

Table 3-26 Correlations and Standardized Regression Coefficients for the Dependent Variable: Change in Percentage of School Revenues from State, 1962 to 1964 (y)

Dependent Variable: Change in percentage of school revenues from state, 1962 to 1964 (y)

Independent Variable	Zero Order Correlation	Standardized Regression Coefficient
Democratic percentage of two-party membership in lower house, 1963–64: x_{16}	.276	.154
Per capita income, 1963: x_{32}	.111	.718
Federal percentage of total welfare expenditures, 1961: x_{98}	.210	.750
Per capita federal grants to state and local governments for health, welfare, and related activities, 1961: x_{81}	.251	.281
Party competition index for lower house, 1963–64: x_{13}	.047	.285

$R = .60^*$ Variance Explained = 39.6%

$$y^{**} = .073x_{16} + .089x_{32} + .329x_{98} + .215x_{81} + .050x_{13} - 439.008$$
$$(.026) \quad (.025) \quad (.098) \quad (.110) \quad (.029)$$

*Significant at the .05 level.

**Regression coefficients unstandardized; standard errors in parentheses.

variable is low $(r = .205)$, and the independent variable fails to emerge in our stepwise regression procedure. All things considered equal, the federal percentage of total welfare expenditures and per capita income emerge as the most positive variables associated with the change. Another welfare variable and two political variables are also positively related to the dependent variable, but all three are very weak correlates. Thus, for this dependent variable prior allocations are relatively unimportant and economic variables are of only secondary importance.

Even more confounding, while expecting prior allocations to be positively associated with change, in Table 3–27 we observe that the change from 1964 to 1965 in the state's share of educational outlays is in fact *negatively* related to the figures for 1964. The variable associated most positively with the change is a welfare variable, namely, general assistance cases as a percentage of the total population.[43]

Turning now to our third dependent variable, we find in Table 3–28 that the change in per capita expenditures for higher education from fiscal 1963 to fiscal 1964 is associated most closely with the comparable figures for 1963—but the relationship is negative. Although in most states the change in expenditures has been in a positive direction, the relationship of prior allocations to the dependent variable indicates that the lower the level of prior expenditures the greater the increase in expenditures. States whose educational expenditures had already attained high levels by 1962 showed disproportionately small increases from 1963 to 1964.

According to Table 3–29, the change in per capita expenditures for higher education from fiscal 1964 to fiscal 1965 is positively correlated with the level of expenditures for 1964 (shown in Table 3–30). The second most important variable within the federalism-and-concern factor is an economic one, namely, state general revenues for 1964. Thus, the variable trends in Table 3–29, unlike those in some earlier tables, do lend support to Proposition 10, which we have been testing.

---

[43] In contrast, the change in per capita educational expenditures of state and local governments is positively related to prior allocations—especially those for 1961. The change in expenditures from 1965 to 1966 is only weakly correlated with prior allocations $(r = .250)$ or change during the last year $(r = .068)$.

Table 3-27 Correlations and Standardized Regression Coefficients for the Dependent Variable: Change in Percentage of School Revenues from State, 1964 to 1965 (y)

Dependent Variable: Change in percentage of school revenues from state, 1964 to 1965 (y)

Independent Variable	Zero Order Correlation	Standardized Regression Coefficient
Percentage of school revenues from state, 1964: x_{135}	−.754	−.645
General assistance cases as a percentage of total population, 1961: x_{99}	.359	.274
Aid to the blind, average monthly payment per recipient, December 1964: x_{53}	.079	−.158
Aid to disabled, recipients per 100,000 population, December 1961: x_{108}	−.161	.243
Democratic percentage of two-party membership in lower house, 1963–64: x_{16}	−.670	−.283

$$R = .85^* \qquad \text{Variance Explained} = 72.2\%$$

$$y^{**} = -.169x_{135} + .112x_{99} - .404x_{53} + .774x_{108} - .047x_{16} + 58.974$$
$$\quad\;\; (.030) \qquad (.036) \qquad (.240) \qquad (.325) \qquad (.021)$$

*Significant at the .01 level.

**Regression coefficients unstandardized; standard errors in parentheses.

Table 3-28 Correlations and Standardized Regression Coefficients for the Dependent Variable: Change in Per Capita Expenditures for Higher Education, 1963 to 1964 (y)

Dependent Variable: Change in per capita expenditures for higher education, 1963 to 1964 (y)

Independent Variable	Zero Order Correlation	Standardized Regression Coefficient
Per capita expenditures for higher education, 1963: x_{55}	−.995	−.995

$$R = .99^* \qquad \text{Variance Explained} = 98\%$$

$$y^{**} = -.9752x_{55} + 37.782$$
$$\quad\;\; (.0136)$$

*Significant at the .001 level.
**Regression coefficients unstandardized; standard errors in parentheses.

Table 3–29 Correlations and Standardized Regression Coefficients for the Dependent Variable: Change in Per Capita Expenditures for Higher Education, 1964 to 1965:y_{55}

Dependent Variable: Change in per capita expenditures for higher education, 1964 to 1965 (y)

Independent Variable	Zero Order Correlation	Standardized Regression Coefficient
Per capita expenditures for higher education, 1964: x_{143}	.415	.384
State general revenues per capita, 1964: x_{44}	.272	.216

$$R = .47^* \qquad \text{Variance Explained} = 22.4\%$$

$$y^{**} = .205x_{143} + .019x_8 + 1.844$$
$$\quad\;\; (.070) \qquad (.012)$$

*Not significant.

**Regression coefficients unstandardized; standard errors in parentheses.

Table 3-30   Correlations and Standardized Regression Coefficients for the Dependent Variable:
Per Capita Expenditures for Higher Education, 1963

Dependent Variable: Per capita expenditures for higher education, 1963: y_{55}

Independent Variable	*Zero Order Correlation*	*Standardized Regression Coefficient*
State general revenues per capita, 1964: x_{44}	.637	.256
State and local expenditures for welfare as a percentage of personal income, 1961: x_{86}	.621	.298
Per capita state expenditures for corrections, 1961: x_{85}	.417	.246
Percentage of state and local revenue from federal government, 1963: x_{43}	.499	.229

$R = .75*$ Variance Explained = 56.5%

$$y** = .4408x_{44} + 3.1381x_{86} + .3132x_{85} + .6024x_{43} - 32.6710$$
$$\quad\;\;(.2660) \quad\quad (1.5386) \quad\quad (.3132) \quad\quad (.3779)$$

*Significant at the .01 level.

**Regression coefficients unstandardized; standard errors in parentheses.

Let us next consider whether current changes in allocations are positively associated with earlier changes in allocations. If they are not, then perhaps we need to develop a new theory regarding state educational allocations.

First let us look at the change in public school expenditures per pupil from fiscal 1964 to fiscal 1965 (see Table 3–31). The pattern that emerges resembles that in Table 3–25. The prior change in expenditures from 1963 to 1964 fails to enter the equation. The correlation between the two periods of change is negative ($r = -.370$), leading us to wonder whether any adequate theory is available to relate earlier changes to current ones.[44]

In viewing the change in the percentage of school revenues derived from the state from 1964 to 1965 (see Table 3–32), the corresponding change from 1962 to 1964 emerges very late in the equation—and even then, the impact is negative. Again, the most important positive variables are welfare and social variables whereas the strongest negative variable is the prior level of allocations. According to our data, the states' share of educational outlays is declining; this decline is emphasized by the negative relationship of prior allocation levels ($r = -.754$) and prior change ($r = -.508$) to this dependent variable. This most recent decline, however, seems to be independent of prior changes or levels since the earlier change for this allocation (from 1962 to 1964) is positively associated with its prior allocation levels ($r = .205$). Thus, it appears that this dependent variable remains sensitive to political shifts whereas other, more obviously economic, outcomes are less susceptible to changing political contexts.[45]

[44] A regression analysis of change was earlier undertaken in a study by Roy W. Bahl, Jr., and Robert J. Saunders, "Determinants of Changes in State and Local Government Expenditures," *National Tax Journal* 18 (March 1965): 50–57. They found that the multiple correlation (i.e., the predictive strength) of the variables declines significantly when prior patterns of change instead of prior allocation levels were used to predict dependent variables. This finding was especially true of educational outcomes.

[45] For the change in the number of students per classroom from 1963 to 1964, the 1963 level is almost perfectly correlated on the negative side ($r = -.999$). As with the state's share of educational expenditures, when subsequent changes in this item are viewed over time prior levels or changes fail to emerge in the regression equation. The change from 1964 to 1965 is negatively associated

Table 3-31   Correlations and Standardized Regression Coefficients for the Dependent Variable: Change in Public School Expenditures Per Pupil, 1964 to 1965 (y)

Dependent Variable: Change in public school expenditures per pupil, 1964 to 1965 (y)

Independent Variable	Zero Order Correlation	Standardized Regression Coefficient
Retail sales per capita, 1963: x_{36}	−.497	−.537
Public school expenditures per pupil, 1963: x_{48}	−.119	1.705
Public school expenditures per pupil, 1964: x_{125}	−.193	−1.233
Democratic percentage of two-party membership in lower house, 1963–64: x_{16}	.420	.263
Per capita state expenditures for correctional system, 1961: x_{85}	−.239	−.287

$$R = .69^* \qquad \text{Variance Explained} = 48.2\%$$

$$y^{**} = -.862x_{36} + .515x_{48} - .328x_{125} + .023x_{16} - .069x_{85} + 97.482$$
$$\quad\;\; (.242) \quad\;\; (.152) \quad\;\; (.134) \quad\;\; (.011) \quad\;\; (.034)$$

*Significant at the .01 level.

**Regression coefficients unstandardized; standard errors in parentheses.

Table 3–32 Correlations and Standardized Regression Coefficients for the Dependent Variable: Change in Percentage of School Revenues from State, 1964 to 1965 (y)

Dependent Variable: Change in percentage of school revenues from state, 1964 to 1965 (y)

Independent Variable	Zero Order Correlation	Standardized Regression Coefficient
Percentage of school revenues from state, 1964: x_{135}	−.754	−.515
General assistance cases as a percentage of total population, December 1961: x_{99}	.359	.209
Aid to the blind, average monthly payment per recipient, December 1964: x_{53}	.079	−.106
Aid to disabled, recipients per 100,000 population, December 1961: x_{108}	−.161	.301
Democratic percentage of two-party membership in lower house, 1963–64: x_{16}	−.670	−.329
Change in percentage of school revenues from state, 1962 to 1964: x_{c1}	−.508	−.128
Average Democratic percentage of gubernatorial elections, 1956–62: x_{97}	−.464	−.377
Negro percentage of population, 1960: x_{20}	−.319	.290

$R = .88*$ Variance Explained = 77.4%

$$y** = -.135x_{135} + .085x_{99} - .271x_{53} + .960x_{108} - .055x_{16} - .119x_{c1} - .152x_{97}$$
$$\ (.032)\quad\ (.035)\quad\ (.239)\quad\ (.329)\quad\ (.020)\quad\ (.081)\quad\ (.061)$$
$$\ + .149x_{97} + 114.866$$
$$\ (-.075)$$

*Significant at the .05 level.

**Regression coefficients unstandardized; standard errors in parentheses.

Observe the stability of the change in per capita expenditures for higher education from fiscal 1964 to 1965 (see Table 3–33). Even though the prior change does not enter the regression equation at all, the prior level of allocations is the strongest positive variable in relation to current change. Past change, while negative, is less forceful in relation to current change ($r = -.275$) than was true of the state's share of educational outlays, considered in the preceding paragraph. Nevertheless, we must conclude (at least for the dependent variables examined) that prior changes in allocations indicate neither the strength nor the direction of current changes.

Thus, our analysis tends to confirm Proposition 10, which stressed the importance of prior allocations, but fails to support Proposition 11. Let us turn now to a more general summary of the findings in this chapter.

Conclusions

Table 3–34 lists by rank of importance the types of independent variables that are related positively to each dependent variable in terms of its standardized regression coefficients. In other words, these are the variables which—all items considered equal—best describe the variance in the particular dependent variable under examination. The table is based on the regression analyses found earlier in the chapter. Let us, then, venture a few conclusions.

1. Educational expenditures in both factors are most closely associated with economic variables, thus confirming Propositions 1 and 10. Political and social variables emerge at only secondary and tertiary levels (as per Corollary 1). These patterns indicate that economic decisions of the legislature are shaped primarily by the economic variables applicable to each state. As the level of wealth, its distribution, and industrial development become more equalized throughout the fifty states, we would expect political variables to

---

with the change from 1963 to 1964 ($r = -.285$) and with the number of students per classroom in 1964 ($r = -.153$). On the whole, the number of students per classroom is declining, but the change is not adequately "explained" by prior levels or changes.

Table 3–33 Correlations and Standardized Regression Coefficients for the Dependent Variable: Change in Per Capita Expenditures for Higher Education, 1964 to 1965 (y)

Dependent Variable: Change in per capita expenditures for higher education, 1964 to 1965 (y)

Independent Variable	Zero Order Correlation	Standardized Regression Coefficient
Per capita expenditures for higher education, 1964: x_{143}	.415	.384
State general revenues per capita, 1964: x_{44}	.272	.216

R = .467*   Variance Explained = 21.8%

$$y** = .205x_{143} + .019x_{44} + 1.844$$
$$\quad\quad (.021) \quad\quad (.012)$$

*Not significant.
**Regression coefficients unstandardized; standard errors in parentheses.

Table 3–34 Rank of Importance of Independent Variables by Type as Related to Dependent Variables

Classification	First	Second	Third
Economic Variables in Static Time Perspective			
Per capita educational expenditures of state and local governments, 1961: y_{73}	Economic	Social	Economic
Noneconomic Variables in Static Time Perspective			
Educational innovation, 1966: y_{124}	Political	Political	Political
American Federation of Teachers membership, June 1966: x_{115}	Social (Urban)	Political	Welfare
National Education Association membership, June 1966: x_{114}	Political		
Percentage of Vocational Act funds allocated to adult education, 1965: y_{120}	Political	Welfare	Economic**
Percentage of Vocational Act funds allocated to postsecondary education, 1965: y_{119}	Economic***	Economic	

Table 3–34 (continued)

Classification	First	Second	Third
Economic Variables Considered Over Time			
Public school expenditures per pupil, 1963: y_{48}	Economic	Economic	Social
Public school expenditures per pupil, 1964: y_{125}	Economic*	Social	Educational
Public school expenditures per pupil, 1965: y_{126}	Economic*	Economic*	Social
Per capita educational expenditures of state and local governments, 1965: y_{127}	Economic*	Social	Economic
Per capita educational expenditures of state and local governments, 1966: y_{128}	Economic*	Social	Economic**
Percentage of school revenues from state, 1964: y_{135}	Political	Political	Political
Percentage of school revenues from state, 1965: y_{136}	Economic*	Political	Political
Per capita expenditures for higher education, 1963: y_{55}	Welfare	Economic	Economic***
Per capita expenditures for higher education, 1964: y_{143}	Social		
Per capita expenditures for higher education, 1966: y_{144}	Economic*	Economic	Economic***
Noneconomic Variables Considered Over Time			
Number of students per classroom, 1964: y_{50}	Political		
Number of students per classroom, 1965: y_{145}	Educational*		
Number of students per classroom, 1966: y_{146}	Educational*	Political	Economic***

Table 3–34 (continued)

Classification	First	Second	Third
Change in Economic Variables Considered Over Time			
Change in public school expenditures per pupil, 1963 to 1964	Economic		
Change in public school expenditures per pupil, 1964 to 1965	Economic*	Economic*	Political
Change in public school expenditures per pupil, 1964 to 1965, considering earlier change, 1963 to 1964	Economic	Political	
Change in percentage of school revenues from state, 1962 to 1964	Welfare	Economic	Political
Change in percentage of school revenues from state, 1964 to 1965	Welfare	Welfare	
Change in percentage of school revenues from state, 1964 to 1965, considering earlier change, 1962 to 1964	Welfare	Social	Welfare
Change in per capita expenditures for higher education, 1963 to 1964	None	Economic	
Change in per capita expenditures for higher education, 1964 to 1965	Economic*	Economic	
Change in per capita expenditures for higher education, 1964 to 1965, considering earlier change, 1963 to 1964	Economic	Economic	

*Prior allocation.

**Gini index, a negative income variable.

***An economic variable based on political decision making.

become increasingly important determinants of economic outcomes. The interplay of executive agencies, interest groups, and constituencies within state legislatures should then become more intense. Indeed, some political variables were not included in Table 3–34 because they had negative regression coefficients; yet, these were Democratic variables and we might have substituted positive Republican variables which would have provided the point that increasing Republican participation at the state level enhances some expenditure patterns.

2. Noneconomic outcomes are primarily dependent upon political and social indicators. Educational innovation, AFT membership, and the distribution of Vocational Act funds typify the trend. Indeed, this finding is one of the most satisfying in the analysis: noneconomic outcomes are related most closely to noneconomic variables (whether social or political), leading us to believe that state legislatures will continue to play a very important role in determining educational outcomes.

3. The percentage of school revenues derived from the state is primarily dependent on political variables, thus disconfirming Proposition 5 and sustaining Corollary 5. Why states fluctuate in their willingness to bear the financial burden of education is a primarily political question.[46]

4. Per capita expenditures for higher education are best predicted by welfare and social variables, even though economic variables provide strong secondary and tertiary support. Thus our analysis tends to disconfirm Proposition 8, which asserted that economic variables would be most important to the determination of this dependent variable.

---

[46] Hofferbert has shown that when such basic indicators as per capita income reach comparably high levels, the allocations within like states vary from a least-squares line. "Ecological Development and Policy Change in the American States," *Midwest Journal of Political Science* 10 (November 1966): 478–80. In effect, as states reach certain development levels, their gross allocations tend to level off. We would expect that when states reach levels of expenditure comparable to their immediate neighbors and to the nation as a whole their contributions to education might well begin to subside. If so, the expansion of educational facilities and services will then become dependent upon locating new local or federal funds. Since the distribution of federal funds will be subject to the same political influences that affect the distribution of state funds, we believe our emphasis upon the legislatures is particularly timely.

5. Political variables best predict the number of students per classroom, thus confirming our expectations in Proposition 9. This conclusion reaffirms the critical nature of state-local relations in that if, for example, state superintendents allow crowded classrooms to predominate in only certain types of schools (e.g., segregated Negro schools in the South) or certain areas of the state, strained relations will inevitably result.

6. As expected, the variables associated with NEA membership are different from those associated with AFT membership.

7. Our analysis strongly supports Proposition 6, which asserted that current educational expenditures would be closely associated with prior allocations. Further, the analysis partially supports Proposition 10, which held that changes in educational expenditures would be explained best by immediate prior allocations. Both of these findings aid in corroborating the assumption implicit in Proposition 7 that independent variables related to a previous outcome would emerge much later, if at all, in the equation for the current outcome.[47]

---

[47] Moreover, this finding is directly in line with the conclusion made by Morss in his review of Sharkansky's work, pp. 95–99. Sharkansky replied to Morss later in "Some More Thoughts About the Determinants of Government Expenditures," *National Tax Journal* 20 (June 1967): 171–79.

chapter 4

Model 2: The Legislative Model

If political variables are important in transforming environmental inputs into educational policy outcomes, then we need to know specifically which variables will "determine" legislators' voting patterns and attitudes toward education. Even though earlier we conceptualized this process in terms of spheres (see Figure 1–2), we might more simply consider voting and attitude formation in linear terms—that is, as a step-by-step process. Figure 4–1 depicts our second model, the legislative model. Farthest from the legislator's vote are the aggregate characteristics of the state—the global and contextual variables. Next in line are the political characteristics of the legislator's district or constituency—the structural variables. Next we focus on the personal characteristics of the legislator—his age, educational background, party affiliation, occupation, and income—which here we label as demographic variables. And lastly, closest to the actual vote, we consider the legislator's attitudes as expressed in the educational issues index, the education lobbyist index, and the legislative process scale.

The reason we are using a linear model now even though earlier we used a sphere model is simple: our techniques for analyzing the data are more suitable to linear than to processual models. When using the latter we could talk about the flowing and overlap between

Figure 4–1
The Legislative Model

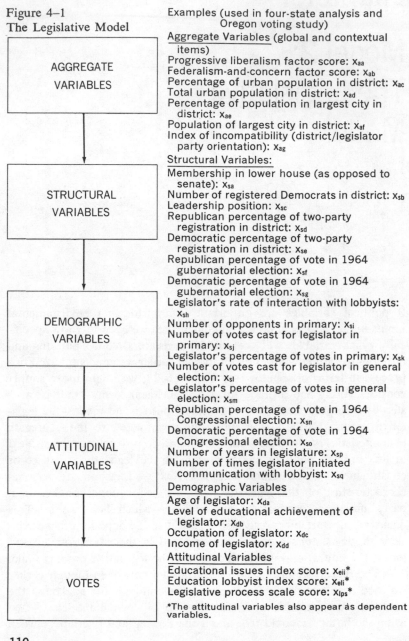

Examples (used in four-state analysis and Oregon voting study)

Aggregate Variables (global and contextual items)

Progressive liberalism factor score: x_{aa}
Federalism-and-concern factor score: x_{ab}
Percentage of urban population in district: x_{ac}
Total urban population in district: x_{ad}
Percentage of population in largest city in district: x_{ae}
Population of largest city in district: x_{af}
Index of incompatibility (district/legislator party orientation): x_{ag}

Structural Variables:

Membership in lower house (as opposed to senate): x_{sa}
Number of registered Democrats in district: x_{sb}
Leadership position: x_{sc}
Republican percentage of two-party registration in district: x_{sd}
Democratic percentage of two-party registration in district: x_{se}
Republican percentage of vote in 1964 gubernatorial election: x_{sf}
Democratic percentage of vote in 1964 gubernatorial election: x_{sg}
Legislator's rate of interaction with lobbyists: x_{sh}
Number of opponents in primary: x_{si}
Number of votes cast for legislator in primary: x_{sj}
Legislator's percentage of votes in primary: x_{sk}
Number of votes cast for legislator in general election: x_{sl}
Legislator's percentage of votes in general election: x_{sm}
Republican percentage of vote in 1964 Congressional election: x_{sn}
Democratic percentage of vote in 1964 Congressional election: x_{so}
Number of years in legislature: x_{sp}
Number of times legislator initiated communication with lobbyist: x_{sq}

Demographic Variables

Age of legislator: x_{da}
Level of educational achievement of legislator: x_{db}
Occupation of legislator: x_{dc}
Income of legislator: x_{dd}

Attitudinal Variables

Educational issues index score: x_{eii}*
Education lobbyist index score: x_{eli}*
Legislative process scale score: x_{lps}*

*The attitudinal variables also appear as dependent variables.

110

the various levels, whereas now we can only "program" a step-by-step progression. Though we are beginning here with a linear model, we do expect that a processual model (or an approximation of one) will emerge during the actual analysis. This will take the form, during our stepwise regression, of certain aggregate variables' explaining most of the variance in a dependent variable, thus appearing first in the regression equation.

Three questions must be answered before considering interactions among the various components of the legislative model:

1. Are regional patterns in educational allocations discernible among the fifty states?
2. Are the four states we have chosen for more detailed analysis, namely, Massachusetts, North Carolina, Oregon, and Utah, generally representative of their respective regions?
3. Are legislators' attitudes and votes more the product of global, analytical, and structural state characteristics than of absolute (i.e., individual) properties?

Regional Differences in Educational Policy Outcomes

Let us consider the first two questions together. In doing so we shall make use of the regression equations developed in Chapter 3 to ascertain the expected values for our various dependent variables in given states. We will then compare the expected value to the observed value in each selected state and a neighboring "control" state and will note whether the two observed values are higher or lower than expected. If our four selected states are generally representative of their regions, they will probably agree with the four respective control states at least a majority of the time.

In Table 4–1 we have indicated whether each of the dependent variables was higher, lower, or about the same as expected in each of our four states and their controls (respectively, Connecticut, South Carolina, Washington, and Arizona). A plus sign (+) denotes a higher value than expected, a minus sign (—) a lower value, and a zero (0) an almost perfect fit. In this way we are able to examine the patterns that emerge across states and presumed regions. Central

Table 4–1 Expected vs. Actual Values for Dependent Variables in Eight Selected States

Classification	Northeast		South		Pacific Northwest		Mountain West	
	Mass.	Conn.	N.C.	S.C.	Oreg.	Wash.	Utah	Ariz.
Economic Variables in Static Time Perspective								
Per capita educational expenditures of state and local governments, 1961: y_{73}	−	−	+	+	+	+	−	+
Noneconomic Variables in Static Time Perspective								
Educational innovation, 1966: y_{124}	−	+	+	+	+	−	+	+
American Federation of Teachers membership, June 1966: y_{115}	−	−	−	−	−	−	−	−
National Education Association membership, June 1966: y_{114}	−	−	+	−	+	+	+	+
Percentage of Vocational Act funds allocated to adult education, 1965: y_{120}	−	−	−	+	−	+	−	−
Percentage of Vocational Act funds allocated to postsecondary education, 1965: y_{119}	−	+	−	−	+	+	+	+
Economic Variables Considered Over Time								
Public school expenditures per pupil, 1963: y_{48}	−	−	+	+	+	−	−	+
Public school expenditures per pupil, 1964: y_{125}	+	−	+	+	+	+	+	−
Public school expenditures per pupil, 1965: y_{126}	−	−	+	−	−	0	−	+

Table 4-1 (continued)

Classification	Northeast		South		Pacific Northwest		Mountain West	
	Mass.	Conn.	N.C.	S.C.	Oreg.	Wash.	Utah	Ariz.
Per capita educational expenditures of state and local governments, 1965: y_{127}	+	+	+	+	+	–	+	–
Per capita educational expenditures of state and local governments, 1966: y_{128}	–	–	–	–	–	–	+	+
Percentage of school revenues from state, 1964: y_{135}	–	+	+	+	+	–	–	+
Percentage of school revenues from state, 1965: y_{136}	+	–	–	+	–	–	–	+
Per capita expenditures for higher education, 1963: y_{55}	–	–	–	–	–	–	+	+
Per capita expenditures for higher education, 1964: y_{143}	+	–	+	–	+	–	+	+
Per capita expenditures for higher education, 1966: y_{144}	+	+	+	+	+	+	+	+
Noneconomic Variables Considered Over Time								
Number of students per classroom, 1964: y_{50}	–	–	0	+	–	–	+	+
Number of students per classroom, 1965: y_{145}	+	–	–	+	–	+	0	+
Number of students per classroom, 1966: y_{146}	+	–	+	–	+	–	+	–
Agreement within region	64.7%		58.8%		58.8%		52.9%	

NOTE: The tables in Appendix B contain the raw data for all of these regression equations.

to this part of our analysis are two assumptions: that the regional pairs will agree a majority of the time and that none of the regions will agree across-the-board with another region on a majority of the items.

For the first set of comparisons, two of our nineteen dependent variables proved insufficiently discriminatory to allow inferences to be drawn from them. Specifically, AFT membership was lower than expected in all eight states; in other words, the regression equation for each of the states predicted a higher level of AFT membership than was observed. Similarly, per capita expenditures for higher education in fiscal 1966 were higher than expected in all eight states.

On the remaining seventeen policy outcomes each regional pair agreed better than a majority of the time with one another. Specifically, Massachusetts and Connecticut were compatible 64.7 percent of the time, North Carolina and South Carolina as well as Oregon and Washington 58.8 percent of the time, and Utah and Arizona 52.9 percent of the time. Upon further examination we find that each state contributes almost equally to the deviance from the trend; in other words, in cases of disagreement the two states have values that are less than expected in about equal proportions.

The percentage of cross-regional agreements on the seventeen variables is computed in Table 4–2. We find that there is only one instance of across-the-board agreement among both the Mountain West and Northeastern states and among the Mountain West and Southern states, and there are only two instances among the Mountain West and Pacific Northwest states. There are four agreements among the Northeastern and Southern states, the Northeastern and Pacific Northwest states, and the Southern and Pacific Northwest states.

Referring back to Table 4–1, we find specifically that the four Mountain West and Northeastern states allocated a smaller percentage of Vocational Act funds to adult education in (fiscal) 1965 than expected. Similarly, the Mountain West and Southern states all scored higher than expected on educational innovation. The four Mountain West and Pacific Northwest states had higher than expected NEA membership figures and greater distributions of Vocational Act funds to postsecondary education than expected.

Continuing the rundown, we find that the Northeastern and

Table 4–2   Cross-Regional Agreements on Expected vs. Actual Values
for the Dependent Variables

	Northeast	South	Pacific Northwest	Mountain West
Northeast				
South	23.5%			
Pacific Northwest	23.5%	23.5%		
Mountain West	5.9%	5.9%	11.8%	

Southern states all show plus signs for the states' percentage of school revenues in 1965 and for the per capita educational expenditures of state and local governments in 1965, whereas they are paired on the minus side on the latter measure for 1966 and on per capita expenditures for higher education in 1963. The four states of the Northeast and Pacific Northwest were below (or even with) their expected allocations for public school expenditures per pupil in 1965, per capita educational expenditures of state and local governments in 1966, and per capita expenditures for higher education in 1963; they also had a smaller than expected student-classroom ratio in 1964. Lastly, our four Southern and Pacific Northwest states all had higher than expected per capita educational expenditures by state and local governments in 1961, higher than expected public school expenditures per pupil in 1964, lower than expected per capita educational expenditures by state and local governments in 1966, and lower than expected per capita expenditures for higher education in 1963.

We may venture a couple of observations about these comparisons. First, let us note that the regional patterns postulated by Sharkansky do in fact emerge here. Second, let us add that the patterns emerging lend weight to Richard Hofferbert's suggestion that poor states compete with one another in attempting to emulate the more developed states.[1]

Next we will compare the readings of our eight states on the nineteen dependent variables with the national mean for each variable.

[1] Richard I. Hofferbert, "Ecological Development and Policy Change in the American States," *Midwest Journal of Political Science* 10 (November 1966): 478.

Table 4–3   Values for Dependent Variables in Eight Selected States in Relation to National Mean

Classification	Northeast		South		Pacific Northwest		Mountain West	
	Mass.	Conn.	N.C.	S.C.	Oreg.	Wash.	Utah	Ariz.
Economic Variables in Static Time Perspective								
Per capita educational expenditures of state and local governments, 1961: y_{73}	−	−	−	−	+	+	+	+
Noneconomic Variables in Static Time Perspective								
Educational innovation: y_{124}	+	+	−	−	+	+	+	+
American Federation of Teachers membership, June 1966: y_{115}	+	+	−	−	−	−	−	−
National Education Association membership, June 1966: y_{114}	−	−	+	−	+	+	+	+
Percentage of Vocational Act funds allocated to adult education, 1965: y_{120}	−	−	−	+	−	+	−	−
Percentage of Vocational Act funds allocated to postsecondary education, 1965: y_{119}	−	+	−	−	+	+	+	+
Economic Variables Considered Over Time								
Public school expenditures per pupil, 1963: y_{48}	+	+	−	−	+	+	−	+
Public school expenditures per pupil, 1964: y_{125}	+	+	−	−	+	+	−	+
Public school expenditures per pupil, 1965: y_{126}	+	+	−	−	+	+	−	+
Per capita educational expenditures of state and local governments, 1965: y_{127}	−	−	−	−	+	+	+	+

Table 4-3 *(continued)*

Classification	Northeast		South		Pacific Northwest		Mountain West	
	Mass.	Conn.	N.C.	S.C.	Oreg.	Wash.	Utah	Ariz.
Per capita educational expenditures of state and local governments, 1966: y_{128}	−	−	−	−	+	+	+	+
Percentage of school revenues from state, 1964: y_{135}	−	−	+	+	−	+	+	−
Percentage of school revenues from state, 1965: y_{136}	−	−	+	+	−	+	+	−
Per capita expenditures for higher education, 1963: y_{55}	−	−	−	−	+	+	+	+
Per capita expenditures for higher education, 1964: y_{143}	+	+	−	−	+	+	+	−
Per capita expenditures for higher education, 1966: y_{144}	+	+	−	−	+	+	+	−
Noneconomic Variables Considered Over Time								
Number of students per classroom, 1964: y_{50}	−	−	+	+	−	−	+	+
Number of students per classroom, 1965: y_{145}	+	−	−	+	−	+	+	+
Number of students per classroom, 1966: y_{146}	+	−	−	+	−	−	+	−
Agreement within region	84.2%		78.9%		78.9%		52.6%	

In Table 4–3 a plus sign indicates a reading above the national mean and a minus sign a reading below the mean. Again, our two assumptions regarding majority agreement are operative. The totals in Table 4–3 indicate that our Northeastern pair of states is easily the most consistent of the four groups, showing 84.2 percent agreement on the nineteen variables; the Southern pair is next with 78.9 percent agreement, as is the Pacific Northwest pair with 78.9 percent agreement, and the two Mountain West states last with a still respectable 52.6 percent agreement. Of the allocation agreements a majority are paired above the national mean in the Pacific Northwest states whereas a majority are below the mean in the Northeastern and Southern states. Within the paired groups, Connecticut, North Carolina, Oregon, and Arizona are usually below the national mean in those instances where they fail to agree with their regional neighbor.

Let us look at the cross-regional comparisons (see Table 4–4) before describing the specific differences within the pairs. The eight agreements between Northeastern and Pacific Northwest states are all plus items except one. The four states (see Table 4–3) were above the national mean for all three variables relating to public school expenditures per pupil, for two dealing with per capita expenditures for higher education, and lastly for the educational innovation variable; their single minus item in common was not really a negative reading in that the four states shared a lower-than-average student-classroom ratio in 1964. A cursory reading of these pairings would suggest that both the Northeast and the Pacific Northwest are definitely pro-education. Further, upon examining the Northeastern pair more closely, we find (excluding the student-classroom ratio variables) that fully one-half of the interstate agreements (eight of sixteen) are minus items, representing readings *below* the national mean, thus forcing us to reconsider our original judgment. The Northeastern and Southern states all have lower-than-average readings for per capita educational expenditures of state and local governments (both in 1961 and 1965), and per capita expenditures for higher education (in 1963). Similarly, the Northeastern and Mountain states agreed only in their sub-par readings on the percentage of Vocational Act funds allocated to adult education.

The four selected Mountain West and Pacific Northwest states agreed on five items. They were above the national mean in all three

Table 4–4   Cross-Regional Agreements on Mean Relationships
of the Dependent Variables

	Northeast	South	Pacific Northwest	Mountain West
Northeast				
South	15.8%			
Pacific Northwest	42.2%	5.3%		
Mountain West	5.3%	15.8%	26.3%	

items relating to per capita educational expenditures of state and local governments and in their NEA membership figures; they lagged below the mean only in their figures for AFT membership. Similarly, the Mountain West and Southern states agreed across-the-board twice, having a more-than-average number of students per classroom in 1964, and a less-than-average AFT membership. Rounding out the picture, the Southern and Pacific Northwest states agreed only in their below-average figures for AFT membership.

A comparison of the national mean with the state mean for each of the nineteen variables shows that the range of variation within each region is very wide (see Table 4–5). For educational policy outcomes we do not find the neat fit that Sharkansky found in his study, in which only 24 of a possible 210 relevant cells varied over 10 percent.[2] In our data 102 of a possible 152 cells vary at least 15 percent from the national mean. Therefore, while Sharkansky is correct in asserting that regional variations do occur, we must conclude that the regional approach may result in information loss because of the necessity of averaging out the variations in educational allocations among the states within each region.

Two more points seem relevant. First, we agree with Hofferbert that

> invidious comparisons with the policy performance of other states (adding to existing internal claims) may be serving as a good to the less developed states. The response is to commit revenues to social

[2] Ira Sharkansky, *Spending in the United States* (Chicago: Rand McNally, 1968), pp. 135–36.

Table 4–5 Deviation from the National Mean of Values for Dependent Variables in Eight Selected States (National Mean = 1.00)

Classification	Northeast		South		Pacific Northwest		Mountain West	
	Mass.	Conn.	N.C.	S.C.	Oreg.	Wash.	Utah	Ariz.
Economic Variables in Static Time Perspective								
Per capita educational expenditures of state and local governments, 1961: x_{73}	.78	.89	.76	.68	1.27	1.29	1.42	1.20
Noneconomic Variables in Static Time Perspective								
Educational innovation, 1966: x_{124}	1.28	1.43	.88	.93	1.13	1.10	1.20	.53
American Federation of Teachers membership, June 1966: x_{115}	1.69	1.29	.00	.00	.26	.50	.00	.44
National Education Association membership, x_{114}	.47	.47	1.24	.84	1.48	1.64	1.37	1.32
Percentage of Vocational Act funds allocated to adult education, 1965: x_{120}	.75	.25	.02	4.51	.20	2.85	.36	2.4
Percentage of Vocational Act funds allocated to postsecondary education, 1965: x_{119}	.12	1.74	.11	.00	1.23	1.74	1.09	2.49
Economic Variables Considered Over Time								
Public school expenditures per pupil, 1963: x_{48}	1.13	1.29	.71	.63	1.25	1.20	.85	1.04
Public school expenditures per pupil, 1964: x_{125}	1.14	1.30	.70	.61	1.23	1.16	.88	1.03
Public school expenditures per pupil, 1965: x_{126}	1.04	1.26	.74	.69	1.21	1.10	.90	1.01

Table 4–5 (continued)

Classification	Northeast		South		Pacific Northwest		Mountain West	
	Mass.	Conn.	N.C.	S.C.	Oreg.	Wash.	Utah	Ariz.
Per capita educational expenditures of state and local governments, 1965: x_{127}	.79	.91	.76	.67	1.33	1.23	1.43	1.20
Per capita educational expenditures of state and local governments, 1966: x_{128}	.76	.86	.78	.67	1.27	1.18	1.46	1.20
Percentage of school revenues from state, 1964: x_{135}	.56	.82	1.76	1.63	.76	1.47	1.21	.84
Percentage of school revenues from state, 1965: x_{136}	.55	.81	1.64	1.48	.66	1.45	1.27	.90
Per capita expenditures for higher education, 1963: x_{55}	.32	.45	.70	.50	1.47	1.42	1.78	1.33
Per capita expenditures for higher education, 1964: x_{143}	2.12	1.04	.94	.55	1.17	1.12	1.56	.93
Per capita expenditures for higher education, 1966: x_{144}	1.98	1.10	.92	.57	1.29	1.14	1.68	.91
Noneconomic Variables Considered Over Time								
Number of students per classroom, 1964: x_{50}	.96	.97	1.00	1.10	.92	.95	1.11	1.02
Number of students per classroom, 1965: x_{145}	1.03	.96	.98	1.10	.92	1.06	1.10	1.04
Number of students per classroom, 1966: x_{146}	1.11	.83	.99	1.10	.98	1.00	1.12	1.00

services "beyond their means," in a sense. That is, the poorer states will tend to devote a higher proportion of their available resources to social services than is the pattern in economically well-off states.[3]

The pattern suggested by Hofferbert does occur, particularly in the South. Even though the two Southern states lagged behind the national mean on most of our nineteen items (see Table 4–3), their actual allocations were quite high in relation to their expected allocations (see Table 4–1). Second, the two states compared within each region manifest expenditure patterns that are surprisingly similar. Across regions, as might be expected, the similarities are less pronounced. For further analysis we have chosen Massachusetts, North Carolina, Oregon, and Utah to represent their respective regions.

Linkages Among the Variables

In moving from aggregate variables to other types of variables we are faced with two questions: (1) Does our theory provide for linking the variables? (2) Can our statistical techniques accommodate the various types of measures associated with the data? Earlier we linked different types of variables conceptually through the economic model (Figure 3–1), a variation on the general political model (Figure 1–1), and later we will examine the legislative model (Figure 4–1) more thoroughly. These models provide the theoretical justification for integrating the different types of data available to us. Let us briefly discuss linkages at this time in order to demonstrate the interconnections between the two models and among the various data levels. This discussion is particularly important since in this study we regard attitudes and votes as subsystem outputs.

Attitudes we regard as outputs of legislators operating in a specified environment. We are concerned not with the specific attitudes of particular legislators but rather with their distribution over the entire group. Votes we regard as structural outputs dependent upon prior interactions between the legislator and his physical and psychological environment.

In our four-state sample global and structural variables together account for only about 9 percent of the variance in the legislators' scores on the educational issues index. In Table 4–6, again basing our

[3] Hofferbert, "Ecological Development and Policy Change," p. 478.

Table 4–6   Correlations and Standardized Regression Coefficients
for the Dependent Variable: Educational Issues Index Score (y)

Dependent Variable: Educational issues index score: y_{eii}

Independent Variable	Zero Order Correlation	Standardized Regression Coefficient
Progressive liberalism factor score: x_{aa}	−.22	−.203
Number of times legislator initiated communication with lobbyists: x_{sq}	−.17	−.088
Membership in lower house: x_{sa}	.10	.074
Leadership position: x_{sc}	.03	.080
Number of opponents in primary: x_{si}	−.17	−.079
Income of legislator: x_{dd}	.09	.056
Republican percentage of vote in 1964 Congressional election: x_{sn}	.03	−.059

$$R^* = .295 \qquad \text{Variance Explained} = 8.7\%$$
$$y^{**} = -.002x_{aa} - .000x_{sq} + .186x_{sa} + .170x_{sc} - .022x_{si}$$
$$\phantom{y^{**} =} (.001) \quad (.000) \quad (.224) \quad (.178) \quad (.025)$$
$$+ .022x_{dd} - .003x_{sn} + 1.117$$
$$ (.032) \quad (.005)$$

*Not significant.
**Regression coefficients unstandardized; standard errors in parentheses.

judgments on the positive strength of the standardized regression coefficients, we find that structural variables are first in order of importance. Thus, whether or not the legislator holds a leadership position and whether he is a member of the lower house or of the senate would be the first variables to control in examining differences in attitudes toward educational issues. The legislator's income, a demographic variable, would be the next item to consider. The strongest negative variable is the state's progressive liberalism factor score. Because of the small percentage of variance explained by the independent variables, however, we must conclude tentatively that these attitudes are less the product of internal legislative or structural influences than of the legislator's personal development.

The education lobbyist index, a measure of the legislator's friendliness toward education lobbyists, is only slightly better defined by global and structural variables (21.3 percent of the variance explained) than the educational issues index (see Table 4–7). When all the variables are controlled, the strongest indicator of a legislator's score on the education lobbyist index is the number of votes he received in the most recent primary. The most significant negative variables are the number of votes cast for the legislator in the general election and the Democratic percentage of his district's 1964 Congressional vote. Thus, competition in the general election is conducive to the formation of friendly attitudes toward education lobbyists, as is, to a smaller extent, Republican registration in a member's district. At the same time, legislators who win conclusively in party primaries tend to be more at ease with education lobbyists than those less sure of their party's nomination. Even so, legislators' attitudes toward education lobbyists are still a highly personal matter, as indicated by the large amount of variance left unexplained.

Even more variance is left unexplained in attempts to predict legislators' scores on the legislative process scale. The two independent variables listed in Table 4–8, namely, the state's federalism-and-concern factor score and the population of the largest city in the member's district, explain only 2 percent of the variance in the dependent variable. Thus, we could predict legislators' scores on the legislative process scale only slightly better by knowing the values of the two independent variables than we could without that knowledge.

Educational Voting Patterns in Oregon

By way of further linking the different types of variables to one another, let us briefly examine the patterns of voting on educational issues in Oregon, the only one of our four states for which we have roll-call votes. Specifically, we have obtained data on twenty-nine education bills that were considered in the 53rd general session of the Oregon legislature. The subject matter of these bills may be classified as follows:

1. Direct expenditures for districts or counties (5 bills).
2. Educational scholarships and loans (2).
3. Vocational schools (1).

Table 4–7   Correlations and Standardized Regression Coefficients
for the Dependent Variable:
Education Lobbyist Index Score (y)

Dependent Variable: Education lobbyist index score: y_{eli}

Independent Variable	Zero Order Correlation	Standardized Regression Coefficient
Leadership position: x_{sc}	−.22	−.067
Federalism-and-concern factor score: x_{ab}	−.17	−.0196
Republican percentage of two-party registration in district: x_{sd}	.11	.038
Number of votes cast for legislator in primary: x_{sj}	.21	1.242
Number of votes cast for legislator in general election: x_{sl}	.10	−1.128
Democratic percentage of vote in 1964 Congressional election: x_{so}	−.05	−.216

$$R^* = .46 \qquad \text{Variance Explained} = 21.3\%$$
$$y^{**} = -.154x_{sc} - .008x_{ab} + .002x_{sd} + .000x_{sj}$$
$$\quad\;\; (.187) \qquad (.004) \qquad (.005) \qquad (.000)$$
$$\quad - .000x_{sl} - .009x_{so} + 1.885$$
$$\quad\;\; (.000) \qquad (.004)$$

*Significant at .001 level.
**Regression coefficients unstandardized; standardized errors in parentheses.

4.   Textbooks (2).
5.   Teacher benefits and certification (8).
6.   School board matters (4).
7.   Administrative functions (4).
8.   Legal matters (3).

For each legislator on each measure we recorded whether he was
a sponsor of the bill (yes = 1, no = 0), whether he voted for the
bill (yes = 1, no = −1, not present or not voting = 0), and whether
the bill passed both houses and was signed by the governor (yes = 1,
no = 0). We were able to compare each legislator's votes on a whole

Table 4–8   Correlations and Standardized Regression Coefficients
for the Dependent Variable:
Legislative Process Scale Score (y)

Dependent Variable: Legislative process scale score: x_{lps}

Independent Variable	Zero Order Correlation	Standardized Regression Coefficient
Federalism-and-concern factor score: x_{ab}	.104	.106
Population of largest city in district: x_{af}	−.091	−.093

$R^* = .14$ Variance Explained = 2%

$$y^{**} = .004x_{ab} - .000x_{af} + 1.234$$
$$(.002) \qquad (.000)$$

---

*Not significant.
**Regression coefficients unstandardized; standard errors in parentheses.

series of bills with those of other legislators, with his factor scores on
a particular pattern of bills, and with other global, structural, and
analytical variables. We conducted our analysis in two steps: first
we examined the rotated factor analysis for consistency among the
bills and then we correlated the legislator's summary scores on these
bills with other variables through regression analysis. The twenty-nine
bills reduced to four major factors that included twenty-one of the
bills and accounted for over 55 percent of the total variance among
the bills. The components of each factor are listed in Table 4–9, and
a description of each follows.

Factor 1:   School Board Power and Citizen Participation

The bipolar first factor indicates that many Oregon legislators
who favor vesting new authority in the school boards prefer at the
same time to maintain some control over who teaches their children.
Teacher retirement plans and the school board's ability to accept
donations are apparently not associated in the members' minds with
improving school systems and support; nor, apparently, is the certification of teachers looked upon with favor by these legislators. One

Table 4–9   Educational Voting Patterns in Oregon, 1965

Factor 1:   School Board Power and Citizen Participation

		Factor Correlation
School boards may purchase property	House Bill 1028	.94
Nomination and selection of Superintendent of Public Instruction	Senate Bill 413	.94
Census-keeping function transferred to higher education	Senate Bill 219	.93
Qualification and election of Superintendent of Public Instruction	Senate Bill 414	.91
Increases general duties of school boards	Senate Bill 248	.70
Recall of school directors (citizen participation)	House Bill 1021	.67
Administration of school district referendum	Senate Bill 6	.65
Establish legalities of new school districts	Senate Bill 243	.55
School board can accept donations	House Bill 1116	−.59
Certification and professionalization of teachers	House Bill 1434	−.63
Retirement of academic employees	House Bill 1247	−.63
Variance Explained = 31.9%		

Factor 2:   Appropriations and Development

Appropriations	House Bill 1095	.85
Appropriations	Senate Bill 38	.84
Appropriations	Senate Bill 32	.83
Increase fund-raising powers of county schools	Senate Bill 85	.71
School board can accept donations	House Bill 1116	−.44
Private vocational school regulation	House Bill 1099	−.45
Variance Explained = 11.8%		

Factor 3:   School Technical Services

School social work	House Bill 1233	.85
Qualifications for school attendance supervisor	House Bill 1024	.64
Private vocational school regulation	House Bill 1099	.56
Variance Explained = 7.8%		

Table 4–9   (*continued*)

Factor 4:   Educational Concern

		Factor Correlation
Remedial care	House Bill 1490	.71
Free textbooks	House Bill 1127	.67
Teachers' tenure provisions	Senate Bill 88	.62
Variance Explained = 5.7%		

---

might assert that Factor 1 is basically antieducational in emphasis, but on checking we find that it is positively correlated with the overall vote on educational issues. (The correlations among the various factors are given in Table 4–10.)

School boards having increased powers to gather resources, members with carefully prescribed qualifications, and a vulnerability to citizen petition can deal more forcefully with teacher, student, or citizen demands. A board can reject claims or rights by virtue of its symbolic subjugation to the will of the people (through the recall and the referendum) when in fact it has real authority vested by law. Overall, then, Factor 1 is progressive in that it places the school board in a competitive position with other governmental units (specifically, the city and the county).

Factor 2: Appropriations and Development

Four of the six items in Factor 2 relate directly to appropriations for schools. Negative orientations toward both school boards' acceptance of donations and private vocational school regulation are associated with a positive stance on expenditures.

Factor 3: School Technical Services

This factor encompasses measures relating to a school social work program, qualifications for an attendance supervisor, and the regulation of private vocational education. A positive score on this factor would seem to indicate favorability toward the professionalization of educational systems.

Table 4–10   Correlations (r) of Votes with the Factor Scores
             Defined by Those Votes

| | Scores on: | | | |
Votes for Issues in:	Factor 1	Factor 2	Factor 3	Factor 4
Factor 1: School Board Power and Citizen Participation	.470	.061	.048	.131
Factor 2: Appropriations and Development	.199	−.082	.166	.039
Factor 3: School Technical Services	−.510	−.179	.190	−.014
Factor 4: Educational Concern	.326	.145	.040	.007
Total Votes for Educational Issues	.220	.027	.158	.104

Factor 4: Educational Concern

All three bills included in Factor 4 met with strong opposition in
the Oregon legislature. They identify a common concern for school
children and employees, for just as free textbooks are important to
families with limited incomes tenure is similarly to teachers who must
live within a limited income range. Employee security is very likely
a key inducement to sustained educational achievement by teachers.

These four factors, which encompass a wide range of educational
issues, reflect different approaches to education on the part of legislators. By means of multiple regression techniques we may now
attempt to explain these four voting patterns by identifying the
analytical, global, and structural variables most important to each of
them.

School Board Power and Citizen Participation

The votes in this pattern are best predicted by the number of
votes cast for the legislator in the preceding primary and by the urban
population of his district (see Table 4–11). In the general election

Table 4–11   Correlations and Standardized Regression Coefficients
for the Dependent Variable: School Board Power
and Citizen Participation (11 Votes)

Dependent Variable: School board power and citizen participation: y_{votes}

Independent Variable	Zero Order Correlation	Standardized Regression Coefficient
Membership in lower house: x_{sa}	.720	.715
Number of votes cast for legislator in primary: x_{sj}	.405	2.877
Number of votes cast for legislator in general election: x_{sl}	.359	−.5514
Total urban population in district: x_{ad}	.339	2.698
Index of incompatibility: x_{ag}	−.117	−.405

$$R^* = .815 \qquad \text{Variance Explained} = 66.4\%$$
$$y^{**} = 46.538x_{sa} + .007x_{sj} - .005x_{sl} + .001x_{ad} - 10.677x_{ag}$$
$$(6.278) \qquad (.002) \qquad (.001) \qquad (.000) \qquad (3.548)$$
$$+ 13.871$$

*Significant at the .001 level.
**Regression coefficients unstandardized; standard errors in parentheses.

(and to some extent in the primary) a large absolute number of votes may be attributable to factors affecting turnout as much or more than it reflects support for the winning candidate. Thus, a large vote does not necessarily give the legislator a sense of independence; it may engender a feeling of caution when the turnout is high and when he receives significant support from members of the opposite party.

The latter situation may be detected by means of an index of legislator-constituency incompatibility. This index reflects the observation that even though state legislators are probably less visible to their voting public than Congressmen,[4] they nonetheless recognize the

[4] Malcolm E. Jewell and Samuel Patterson, *The Legislative Process in the United States* (New York: Random House, 1966), pp. 341 and 343–52; and John C. Wahlke, Heinz Eulau, William Buchanan, and LeRoy Craig Ferguson, *The Legislative System* (New York: John Wiley, 1962), pp. 294–308.

possibility of retaliation by the public on election day.[5] From the fore-going we may infer that a legislator would less likely vote the straight party line on any bill or group of bills if he expected his actions to have severe negative repercussions in the next election.

Constituency incompatibility is a measure of the extent to which party registration figures or party vote for governor or Congressman are inconsistent with the party affiliation of the legislator.[6] A high score on the index indicates a high level of incompatibility between the legislator's party affiliation and the partisan complexion of his district. We find that the index is negatively related to this particular complex of votes—a not surprising finding in that Factor 1, after all, does include issues relating to citizen control of education. It seems plausible to suggest that the greater the political incompatibility be-tween a legislator and his constituents, the less likely he would be to support measures increasing their control over education.

Thus, party competition and urbanization are important in ex-plaining this voting pattern. In addition, membership in the lower house has a positive bearing on these votes. Senate membership may be a structural variable that intervenes between the legislator's vote and his constituency in Oregon, much as it does in Pennsylvania.[7]

Appropriations and Development

The variable contributing most to positive votes on appropriations and development is a measure of urbanization, specifically, the per-centage of urban population in the district (see Table 4–12). Re-publican registration in the district is also positively correlated with the pattern. In addition, lower house membership and the percentage of the legislator's vote in the general election are positive correlates. On the other hand, high educational levels among the legislators, high levels of Democratic registration and incompatibility (as previously

[5] Robert A. Dahl and Charles E. Lindblom, *Politics, Economics and Welfare* (New York: Harper and Row, 1953), p. 313.

[6] See further, Michael Baer, "Environmental Effects on State Legislators and Lobbyists" (Ph.D. dissertation, University of Oregon, 1968), pp. 152–53.

[7] See Thomas R. Dye, "A Comparison of Constituency Influences in the Upper and Lower Chambers of a State Legislature," *Western Political Quarterly* 14 (June 1961): 474–78.

Table 4–12   Correlations and Standardized Regression Coefficients
for the Dependent Variable:
Appropriations and Development (6 Votes)

Dependent Variable: Appropriations and development: y_{votes}

Independent Variable	Zero Order Correlation	Standardized Regression Coefficient
Membership in lower house: x_{sa}	.331	.228
Index of incompatibility: x_{ag}	−.197	−.048
Republican percentage of two-party registration in district: x_{sd}	.111	.536
Democratic percentage of two-party registration: x_{se}	.060	−.559
Legislator's level of educational achievement: x_{db}	−.092	−.332
Percentage of urban population in district: x_{ac}	.066	.642
Number of opponents in primary: x_{si}	.006	−.428
Number of years in legislature: x_{sp}	.196	−.234
Legislator's percentage of votes in general election: x_{sm}	.052	.260

$$R^* = .481 \qquad \text{Variance Explained} = 23.1\%$$
$$y^{**} = 9.247x_{sa} - 7.697x_{ag} + .942x_{sd} - .828x_{se} - 4.183x_{db}$$
$$(.6284) \quad (3.562) \quad (.439) \quad (.464) \quad (2.352)$$
$$+ .496x_{ac} - 1.919x_{si} - 1.075x_{sp} + .306x_{sm} + 88.288$$
$$(.280) \quad (1.265) \quad (.940) \quad (.329)$$

*Not significant.
**Regression coefficients unstandardized; standard errors in parentheses.

defined) in the district, legislative tenure, and opposition in the primary all tend to militate against positive votes on appropriations.

If our later findings on attitudes fail to bear out our findings here, we might conclude that behavioral performance (i.e., voting) is relatively unrelated to attitudes. For example, we have just observed that Oregon legislators' level of educational achievement is negatively correlated with votes for educational appropriations; yet, if we later find that the level of education is positively associated with favorable attitudes toward education, we will have to conclude that intervening considerations apparently override these predispositions.

Interestingly, while the variables in the regression equation accounted for nearly two-thirds of the variance in the first factor, they are unable to explain more than a quarter of the variance in Factors 2, 3, and 4.

School Technical Services

The legislator's income, his age, and a high score on the educational issues index are all associated with positive votes in this pattern (see Table 4–13). We might say that high scores on this factor reflect the legislator's independence and judgment, for analytical characteristics such as income, personal beliefs, and (the wisdom that comes with) age are the only variables that can override the negative effects of structural variables like party competition and urbanization. Our analysis also indicates that the legislator scoring high on this factor tends to avoid contact with education lobbyists and with lobbyists in general.

Educational Concern

In Table 4–14 we find that the voting pattern expressing concern for school children and teachers is positively related to support in the primary and (by deduction from the index of incompatibility) in the general election. The negative effects of tenure, however, may offset the positive contributions of these two variables. For example, whenever the issue of free textbooks comes before the Oregon legislature, well-tenured members with strong constituency support usually vote against the bill. The global, structural, and analytical variables that we have examined are unable to explain this pattern of.voting.

We might hypothesize that these legislators are from districts where party competition is keen and where the index of incompatibility is low.[8] Charisma, personal orientations toward public welfare, the legislator's occupation, and self-interest motives are all potential con-

---

[8] See Jewell and Patterson, *The Legislative Process,* pp. 349–52.

Table 4–13   Correlations and Standardized Regression Coefficients
             for the Dependent Variable:
             School Technical Services (3 Votes)

Dependent Variable: School technical services: y_{votes}

Independent Variable	Zero Order Correlation	Standardized Regression Coefficient
Income of legislator: x_{dd}	.202	.311
Legislative process scale score: x_{lps}	−.195	−.247
Legislator's rate of interaction with lobbyists: x_{sh}	−.134	−.131
Population of largest city in district: x_{af}	−.061	−.227
Education lobbyist index score: x_{eli}	−.098	−.167
Age of legislator: x_{da}	−.159	.198
Number of years in legislature: x_{sp}	−.011	−.178
Educational issues index score: x_{eii}	.116	.112
Legislator's percentage of votes in primary: x_{sk}	−.105	−.169
Number of votes cast for legislator in primary: x_{sj}	−.077	−.143

$$R^* = .480 \qquad \text{Variance Explained} = 23.0\%$$
$$y^{**} = 3.1667x_{dd} - 7.267x_{lps} - 4.492x_{sh} - .000x_{af} - 3.296x_{eli}$$
$$\quad (1.546) \qquad (4.376) \qquad (5.313) \qquad (.000) \qquad (.2798)$$
$$\quad - 4.279x_{da} + 1.034x_{sp} + 2.795x_{eii} - 2.490x_{sk} - .000x_{sj}$$
$$\quad (3.565) \qquad (.979) \qquad (3.589) \qquad (2.552) \qquad (.000)$$
$$\quad + 49.147$$

*Not significant.
**Regression coefficients unstandardized; standard errors in parentheses.

siderations, but these are not measured in our study. Nonetheless, our results are not so gloomy as this single educational voting pattern in Oregon might indicate. Later in this chapter we will be examining patterns of educational support in our four selected states, and we will at that time venture additional conclusions regarding the variables most important to educational policy outcomes.

For now we may say that independent variables considered im-

Table 4–14   Correlations and Standardized Regression Coefficients
              for the Dependent Variable:
              Educational Concern (3 Votes)

Dependent Variable: Educational concern: y_{votes}

Independent Variable	Zero Order Correlation	Standardized Regression Coefficient
Number of votes cast for legislator in primary: x_{sj}	.189	.264
Education lobbyist index score: x_{eli}	.143	.232
Number of years in legislature: x_{sp}	−.095	−.255
Index of incompatibility: x_{ag}	−.108	−.192

$$R^* = .358 \qquad \text{Variance Explained} = 12.8\%$$
$$y^{**} = .001x_{sj} + 3.584x_{eli} - 1.155x_{sp} - 3.127x_{ag} + 60.372$$
$$(.000) \quad (2.134) \qquad (.679) \qquad (2.368)$$

*Not significant.
**Regression coefficients unstandardized; standard errors in parentheses.

portant for later examination include legislative interaction, party competition, and legislators' views as reflected in our three attitudinal indices. Describing the legislator's setting (i.e., the state political environment) seems the most appropriate way of approaching an explanation of the legislator's general orientation. More detailed studies will be needed to discern differences among legislators based on competition in both primaries and general elections, on constituency and party orientations, and on urban-rural differences. Tentatively urbanization may be measured by a district's density of population and its urban population percentage.

If the preceding discussion seems to suggest that we can infer individual behavior from global or structural data, let us here reassure the reader that this is not so. In focusing upon Oregon we were trying to explain an individual's activity as traced strictly in group terms within a legislative setting. In our analysis we regard the individual *qua* individual as relatively unimportant. Far more important are the distribution and aggregation of activities among individuals, for in breaking variables into the structural and absolute categories of relational, demographic, and attitudinal variables (as we do in the legislative model) we are using individual legislators simply to provide the raw material for subsequent analysis.

In addition, our conversion of legislators' beliefs into attitude scales makes possible analysis at a level not previously possible. Therefore, it is important for us to ask how attitudes are related to structural or relational variables. One possibility that we should consider is that education lobbyists may effectuate changes in legislators' attitudes toward educational policy outcomes.

Legislators' Interaction with Education Lobbyists

One major element in effective lobbying consists in locating the right target. Calculating the number of contacts a given lobbyist has with legislators tells us nothing about the relative importance of these contacts. *Who* a lobbyist contacts is often more important than the frequency of the contacts. In this section we wish to inquire whether education lobbyists are effective in communicating their objectives to legislators. More specifically, we shall ask whether legislators feel pressured by lobbyists, which groups (education lobbyists or business lobbyists) they prefer to consult with regarding the education budget, and how often they discuss educational matters with each group. Legislators generally prefer formal committee meetings or appointments with lobbyists as means of channeling interactional contacts in the legislative structure.[9] Let us now consider whether legislators discuss educational matters more often with education lobbyists than with business lobbyists, who, after all, constitute the majority of all lobbyists.[10]

In each of the four states studied the legislators perceived pressure from lobbyists, but this perception did not necessarily influence the frequency of their contacts with the two groups of lobbyists. Legislators consult business leaders about the education budget for

[9] See Harmon Zeigler and Michael Baer, *Lobbying: Interaction and Influence in the State Legislature* (Belmont, Calif.: Wadsworth, 1969), Chapter 8.
[10] *Ibid.*, pp. 109–14 and 117–20.

at least two good reasons: (1) to determine the effects of an increased educational budget on various businesses and relevant tax structures, and (2) to ascertain the views of cohorts and associates, since businessmen constitute the largest occupational grouping within the legislature.

Regardless of perceptions of pressure, we expected that members of both parties would consult education lobbyists on matters of particular relevance to education. We find that—to a surprising degree—legislators also contact business lobbyists, other legislators, and (to a lesser extent) party officials and government officials on educational matters. In each of the four states contact with interest groups was greater among legislative leaders than among the rank-and-file membership. Even when the leaders show a marked reluctance to contact certain groups (as is true of the Democratic leaders in Oregon), this reluctance is accentuated among the followership. Education lobbyists, while somewhat more effective than other lobbyists in consulting with legislators on matters vital to themselves, are still not the group most often contacted by legislators. As Table 4–15 shows, business lobbyists enjoy a much higher rate of return on their initiated contacts with legislators than do education lobbyists.

Only in North Carolina, where the Democratic legislators far outnumber their Republican counterparts, are the Democrats more apt to regard education lobbyists as a pressure group than the Republicans. In Oregon and to a lesser extent in Massachusetts and Utah, Republicans are more sensitive than Democrats to education lobbyists' pressures.

Might legislators' perceptions of pressure from education lobbyists be associated with declining solicitations from legislators during the legislative session? Surprisingly, we find that the legislators who perceive pressure from education lobbyists are those most willing to solicit contacts with lobbyists. There appears to be a fine line of distinction between persuasion and pressure that can be exploited handsomely by those personally acquainted with legislators. Personal acquaintance or friendship makes the lobbyists' pressuring appear less noxious or menacing. Lobbyists who were formerly legislators can use their prior associations and connections with colleagues still in the legislature to great effect; they can also expect legislators to seek their advice and counsel more frequently on matters of mutual concern.

Table 4-15   Legislators' Perceptions of Contacts with Lobbyists:
              Number of Contacts Per Week from Lobbyists
              vs. Number of Contacts Per Session Initiated by Legislators

	Massachusetts		North Carolina		Oregon		Utah	
	r	N	r	N	r	N	r	N
Education lobbyists	.304	20	.077	10	.000	4	.196	22
Business lobbyists	.636	94	.505	71	.661	97	.626	46
Labor lobbyists	.000	4	1.000	4	.779	6	.200	5
Other lobbyists	.770	31	.316	28	.706	43	.698	35

Thus, we expect that a lobbyist with prior legislative experience usually can sway a legislator to his point of view than can a lobbyist with no prior legislative experience—all without seeming to pressure so much as to persuade.

The distinction between pressure and persuasion bears directly on the legislator's perception of lobbyists in relation to an "unwritten code of ethics." We would expect that legislators who regard lobbyists as the lackeys of pressure groups might well be hesitant to believe that lobbyists follow an unwritten code of ethics. In our four-state sample we find that only in Massachusetts do the legislators doubt the consistent operation of such a code ($r = -.41$, Sign. $= .01$).[11] Within all the states where pressure is perceived most legislators believe that lobbyists follow an unwritten code of ethics. Again we would suggest that the knowledge gained by having formerly been a legislator or, alternatively, a government official helps the perceptive lobbyist read the legislature's feeling about a bill or issue. Though legislators might well cite several groups as pressure groups, simultaneously they could also perceive an unwritten code of ethics generally operative among the lobbyists.

In states where an ethical code was truly functioning we would expect to find few bribery attempts in the legislature. We can test this

[11] *Ibid.,* pp. 70–74.

hypothesis by asking legislators who perceive direct pressure from education lobbyists and those who do not whether they also know of any bribes attempted within their body by lobbyists (hoping with this question to pick up a consistent attitude of hostility toward not only education lobbyists but lobbyists in general).

In North Carolina and Utah we find that legislators who perceive pressure from education lobbyists tend quite strongly also to remember some bribery attempts within the legislature. This tendency is considerably weaker in Oregon and nonexistent in Massachusetts. In Massachusetts, where legislator-lobbyist contact is very formalized and remote, not a single legislator who perceived education lobbyists as a pressure group was able to remember a bribery attempt. In Utah, a state traditionally hostile to educational interests, and in North Carolina, a state run by what one might call an oligarchy,[12] we discovered a definite hostility toward interests regarded as pressure groups.

Logically, we might expect negative feelings toward groups regarded as pressure-oriented to be reflected in negative attitudes toward their interests in the legislature. For example, we might expect that legislators' attitudes about previous education budgets would be affected negatively to the extent that the legislators perceived the education lobbyists as being prone to pressure tactics. However, these expectations remain unfulfilled. We find that most legislators are inclined to be satisfied with the education budget for the previous year *regardless of their perceptions of pressure.*[13] Specifically, we find that 73 percent of the "pressured" legislators are satisfied with the previous year's education budget, as compared to only 63 percent of those who detected no pressure. Surprisingly enough, of the 27 percent dissatisfied with the budget who perceive pressure in education lobbyists' activities, a majority believe that the education budget should be larger. As expected, "unpressured" legislators are also more likely than not to believe that the budget should be larger ($r = -.41$, Sign. $= .05$).

[12] V. O. Key, Jr., *Southern Politics* (New York: Vintage Books, 1949), pp. 211–15.

[13] See LeRoy Craig Ferguson, *How State Legislators View the Problem of School Needs* (East Lansing, Mich.: Cooperative Research Projects, Michigan State University, 1960), Project No. 532, pp. 37–43.

Thus, generally we can more accurately predict the direction of a state's education budget by knowing whether or not its legislators regard education lobbyists as a pressure group. Instead, upon examining individual states, we find that the patterns are mixed. In North Carolina and Oregon the legislators satisfied with the previous year's education budget are generally those who feel pressured by education lobbyists, whereas in Massachusetts and Utah those *dissatisfied* with the budget are drawn disproportionately from the pressured group. In the last two states most of the legislators satisfied with the previous year's budget did not feel pressured by education lobbyists. Only in Utah did we find that unpressured legislators tended to believe that the education budget should have been larger, whereas in the three other states it was predominantly the pressured legislators who believed that the budget should have been larger.

Next we will examine particular variables to see whether they help to explain legislators' attitudes toward educational issues and education lobbyists. In particular, we shall relate variables concerned with party affiliation, leadership status, party competition, political incompatibility within the district, and urbanization to the three attitudinal indices already developed, namely, the educational issues index, the education lobbyist index, and the legislative process scale. For our present purposes we have divided the indices into high-low and high-medium-low categories in order to posit our analysis at the ordinal level. Table 4–16 shows the distribution of the scores on these indices among the 582 state legislators interviewed. A low score on the education lobbyist index indicates little support for educational interests, whereas a low score on the legislative process scale denotes a lack of support for lobbyists in general.

Party Affiliation

Do legislators' party affiliations affect educational policy outcomes? Malcolm E. Jewell and Samuel Patterson have noted that the "broad category of issues on which party cohesion is high includes health, education, and welfare services, all kinds of labor legislation . . . and measures to regulate business."[14] Thomas Dye, on the other hand,

[14] Jewell and Patterson, *The Legislative Process,* p. 431.

Table 4–16   Distribution of Legislators' Scores
on Attitudinal Indices

	Educational Issues Index (Mean = 1.864)	Education Lobbyist Index (Mean = 1.751) (N = 582)	Legislative Process Scale (Mean = 1.412)
High	27.8%	55.3%	33.3%
Medium	37.1%		
Low	27.8%	44.7%	66.7%

perceives "no independent relationship between partisanship" and educational public policy.[15] Supporting this view is LeRoy Craig Ferguson's observation that in Tennessee, California, Ohio, and New Jersey, Republican and Democratic legislators agreed on school needs more than 50 percent of the time.[16] John C. Wahlke and his colleagues suggest that there is a "present need of research into the roles of legislators as party members."[17] In this section we shall examine whether party affiliation is an important variable in the institutional context of the individual legislator.

In Pennsylvania, notes Frank J. Sorauf, the Democratic party has demonstrated a degree of party discipline unmatched by that of the Republicans.[18] While agreeing with Sorauf's observation that most legislation is handled on a nonpartisan basis in Pennsylvania,[19] William J. Keefe nonetheless found a strong split between Democrats and Republicans on tax matters. Specifically, the Democrats opposed an income tax bill backed by the Pennsylvania State Education

[15] Thomas R. Dye, "Policy Outcomes in Public Education" (mimeographed paper presented at the Conference on Politics and Education, Center for the Advanced Study of Educational Administration, University of Oregon, 1966), p. 30.

[16] Ferguson, How Legislators View School Needs, pp. 34–35.

[17] Wahlke et al., The Legislative System, pp. 34–35.

[18] Frank J. Sorauf, Party and Representation (New York: Atherton Press, 1963), pp. 137–39.

[19] William J. Keefe, "Parties, Partisanship, and Public Policy in the Pennsylvania Legislature," American Political Science Review 48 (June 1954): 452.

Society, the governor, and the Republican party on the grounds that it was not graduated like the federal income tax.[20]

First let us ask whether Democratic legislators are more inclined to favor educational expenditures and increased taxes than their Republican counterparts. The usual assumption, scarcely ever called into question, is that Democrats are generally more favorable to public policies relating to health, education, and welfare than Republicans. Table 4–17, which gives a detailed breakdown of the responses to two questions in the educational issues index, indicates that the legislator's party affiliation only marginally affects his views on educational matters. In Massachusetts both Democrats and Republicans overwhelmingly believed that the proportion of expenditures for education will increase, and both groups favored a tax increase for education. Not a single Utah legislator thought that education's share of the budget would decrease, but more than one-fifth of the members were satisfied with the present levels of expenditure. Also, Utah legislators were the only group of the four to oppose additional taxes for education, opposition running particularly strong among the Republican members. The patterns were mixed in the other two states. In North Carolina Democratic legislators were more inclined to anticipate increased educational expenditures than the Republicans, whereas in Oregon the reverse was true. Conversely, North Carolina Republicans and Oregon Democrats favored a tax increase for education slightly more than their counterparts. Overall, our figures suggest that in states statistically favorable to education one will likely find both parties favorable to educational interests. Obviously, other comparative studies will be necessary to describe the varieties of educational attitudes in relation to party affiliations.

The highly positive responses of Massachusetts legislators doubtless reflect that state's longtime concern with quality education, both in public and private schools. Other historical circumstances inevitably intrude upon our interpretation of the figures. At the time of this survey, for example, North Carolinians had just experienced a controversy concerning the right of radical figures to speak at state universities. Similarly, in Utah the National Education Association had recently investigated contract problems concerning elementary

[20] *Ibid.,* p. 456.

Table 4–17 Comparison of Republican and Democratic Legislators on Two Educational Issues

Question: Do you think that the proportion of expenditures for education will increase, decrease, or remain the same?

Question: Would you favor or oppose a tax increase for education?

Percentage who believe the proportion for education will:

	Mass.		N.C.		Oreg.		Utah		Total	
	Rep.	Dem.	Rep.	Dem.	Rep.	Dem.	Rep.	Dem.	Rep.	Dem.
Increase	97.0	97.0	73.3	86.5	87.5	76.7	76.4	81.6	88.9	89.0
Decrease	0.0	.6	13.3	2.0	2.5	6.9	0.0	0.0	2.0	2.0
Remain the same	3.0	2.4	13.3	11.5	10.0	16.2	23.6	18.4	10.0	9.0
N =	74	162	15	148	40	43	38	49	167	401

Percentage who favor a tax increase for education (remainder oppose an increase):

	Rep.	Dem.	Rep.	Dem.	Rep.	Dem.	Rep.	Dem.	Rep.	Dem.
	86.0	73.3	64.3	56.7	54.0	65.0	9.5	34.7	61.0	61.0
N =	71	152	14	143	37	40	36	49	158	384

NOTE: Percentage figures may not always total 100.0% because of rounding.

and secondary school teachers.[21] At the time of our study Oregonians were attempting to raise taxes to pay for increased school expenditures, and a strong group advocating limits on the property tax was pressing the legislature for relief. Thus we see that survey results must be interpreted in the light of traditions and recent historical development if we are to understand properly the phenomena under scrutiny.

Related to this concern with partisan influences is the study of legislative leadership roles,[22] for whichever party holds the largest number of seats in the legislature controls committee chairmanships and—theoretically, at least—a majority of the votes.

Leaders vs. Followers

Leadership roles, being part of the collective properties of the legislature, are occupied by members related in specified ways to one another; that is, the roles are designated by specific party action and are accompanied by certain expectations on the part of all concerned. Of course there are certain informal factors such as kinship, friendship, expertise, ideology, or area that may be important in one or another situation,[23] but these are not of prime concern here. Nor are we concerned primarily in this study with interactions *per se*, there being well over twenty-eight thousand possible dyadic pairs in the Massachusetts house alone. We merely wish briefly to discuss formal, ascribed leadership and leader-follower relationships in respect to legislators' attitudes toward education.

On the national level, Herbert McClosky and his associates have observed not only significant differences between the leaders and followers in the same party but also different patterns between the

[21] See John C. Evans, Jr., *Utah School Crisis, 1963* (Salt Lake City, Utah: Utah Education Association, 1963); and National Education Association, *Utah: A State-Wide Study of School Conditions* (Washington, D.C.: National Commission on Professional Rights and Responsibilities, 1964).

[22] Austin Ranney, "Parties in State Politics," in *Politics in the American States* (Boston: Little, Brown, 1965), pp. 61–99.

[23] Heinz Eulau *et al.,* "Career Perspectives of American State Legislators," in *Political Decision-Makers,* ed. Dwaine Marvick (Glencoe, Ill.: The Free Press, 1961), pp. 13–14.

two parties.[24] In respect to educational values, McClosky found that in both parties followers favored increases in federal aid to education in significantly greater percentages than leaders.[25] LeRoy Ferguson's study, while covering party, strength of party, and representational roles in relation to educational attitudes, failed to take up formal leadership roles.[26]

For our purposes we define role as "behavioral consistencies on the part of one person as he contributes to a more or less stable relationship with one or more others."[27] For every leader there is a prescribed way of behaving: his position defines his role. Thus, roles have a very definite meaning in the legislative context in this study. We may ask, Does a legislator's leadership role automatically differentiate him from other legislators? Remember that we are here treating strictly formal leadership roles (as exemplified by the positions of Speaker, committee chairman, floor leader, and party whip), not informal leadership roles.[28]

Drawing on our earlier discussions, we would suggest that, on the whole, followers will be more favorable toward educational expenditures and taxes than leaders. This greater degree of conservatism on the part of leaders is implied by the neutral position expected of a leader and is confirmed by McClosky's findings. In Table 4–18 we can see that Republican legislative leaders are generally less enthusiastic about providing new taxes to pay for anticipated increases in educational expenditures than nonleaders (the sole exception being in Massachusetts). A similar pattern prevails among the Democrats (Utah being the sole exception). Thus, our expectations are con-

[24] Herbert McClosky et al., "Issue Conflict and Consensus Among Party Leaders and Followers," American Political Science Review 54 (June 1960): 413.

[25] Ibid., pp. 422–23.

[26] Ferguson, How Legislators View School Needs, pp. 66–67; yet see Eulau et al., "Career Perspectives," pp. 170–92.

[27] Theodore M. Newcomb, Ralph H. Turner, and Philip E. Converse, Social Psychology (New York: Holt, Rinehart & Winston, 1960), p. 323.

[28] The close interrelationship between informal and formal leadership roles is well documented, however, in Samuel C. Patterson, "Patterns of Interpersonal Relations in a State Legislature Group: The Wisconsin Assembly," Public Opinion Quarterly 23 (Spring 1959): 101–9.

Table 4–18 Comparison of Legislative Leaders and Nonleaders on Two Educational Issues

Percentage who believe the proportion of expenditures for education will:	Mass.		N.C.		Oreg.		Utah		Total	
	L	N = L	L	N = L	L	N = L	L	N = L	L	N = L
Republicans										
Increase	100.0	96.5	50.0	81.8	83.8	100.0	75.0	76.7	84.8	89.8
Decrease	0.0	0.0	0.0	18.2	3.2	0.0	0.0	0.0	1.7	1.9
Remain the same	0.0	3.4	50.0	0.0	13.0	0.0	25.0	23.3	13.5	8.3
N =	16	58	4	11	31	9	8	30	59	108
Democrats										
Increase	96.8	98.5	84.0	90.7	75.8	78.5	82.0	80.0	87.5	92.4
Decrease	1.0	0.0	3.2	0.0	10.3	0.0	0.0	0.0	2.7	0.0
Remain the same	2.2	1.5	12.8	9.2	13.8	21.5	18.0	20.0	9.8	7.6
N =	95	66	94	54	29	14	39	10	257	144
Percentage who favor a tax increase for education:										
Republicans	92.9	84.3	0.0	90.0	51.8	62.5	0.0	25.0	51.0	67.0
N =	14	57	4	10	29	8	8	28	55	103
Democrats	70.5	75.0	48.9	69.9	55.5	84.6	38.4	20.0	55.8	70.0
N =	88	64	90	53	27	13	39	10	244	140

firmed: legislative leaders are more conservative on these two questions than the rank-and-file members. Again, Massachusetts and Utah legislators are at the extremes. While both groups anticipate increased educational expenditures, Utah legislators strongly oppose tax increases for education.

Broadening our analysis through the use of the three attitudinal indices discussed earlier, we discover the patterns shown in Table 4–19. As expected, nonleaders are more favorable to educational issues in general than the leadership element (the sole exception being in Utah, where there is no discernible trend). Surprisingly, though leaders are generally more favorable toward education lobbyists than nonleaders, as indicated by the second of our indices. By concentrating their energies on legislative leaders rather than on the rank-and-file membership, lobbyists may be largely wasting their time; for leaders are evidently more receptive to education lobbyists personally than to the policies they espouse. The contrast in scores on the education lobbyist index is particularly striking among Oregon and North Carolina legislators.

This last point on leader disposition is explicitly brought out in the leaders' more conservative stance on the legislative process scale. Among the four groups, North Carolina legislative leaders shift the most dramatically between the second and third measures, indicating their general suspicion of lobbyists. In North Carolina education lobbyists, while receiving some support from legislative leaders, do not operate in a friendly atmosphere; and rarely do they receive strong support for their legislative proposals.

Party Competition in the Legislator's District

Both Heinz Eulau and Malcolm E. Jewell have noted that the electoral complexion of districts changes from one election to the next and that measures of party competition tend to obscure these variations.[29] Because of the constant shifting of populations and of district boun-

---

[29] Eulau et al., "Career Perspectives," p. 222; and Malcolm E. Jewell, *Legislative Representation in the Contemporary South* (Durham, N.C.: Duke University Press, 1967), p. 12.

Table 4–19   Comparison of Legislative Leaders and Nonleaders
              on Attitudinal Indices

		Leaders (N = 320)	Nonleaders (N = 258)
Educational Issues Index			
	High	26.2%	32.9%
x^2 = 6.09, Sign. = .05	Medium	36.7	41.9
gamma = −.17, Sign. = .001	Low	34.1	25.2
Education Lobbyist Index			
x^2 = 9.53, Sign. = .002	High	61.3%	41.8%
gamma = .26, Sign. = .001	Low	38.7	51.9
Legislative Process Scale			
x^2 = .004, Sign. = NS	High	33.4%	33.3%
gamma = .002, Sign. = NS	Low	66.6	66.7

daries, measures of party competition will not necessarily dominate the legislators' views on public policy. Of course, indices may be constructed to reflect electoral data over a period of many years.[30] However, our research requires the devising of an index that reflects the legislator's current perception of his constituency in relation to educational matters. Since trend data does not reflect the immediacy of the elections, we have combined the following three indicators to construct our own index of party competition:

1. The legislator's percentage of votes in the most recent general election.
2. The legislator's percentage of votes in the latest primary.
3. A supplementary indicator to introduce interparty competition (for North Carolina and Utah, the results of the most recent gubernatorial and congressional elections; for Oregon and Massachusetts, party registration figures).[31]

[30] See Ranney, "Parties in State Politics," pp. 85–86; and Jewell, *Representation in the South*, p. 12.

[31] If the party registration figures or the winning majority was less than 53 percent for either party, the district was summarily expelled from considera-

Table 4–20 Comparison of Legislators from Competitive and Noncompetitive Districts on Two Educational Issues

Percentage who believe the proportion of expenditures for education will:	Mass.		N.C.		Oreg.		Utah		Total	
	C	N=C	C	N=C	C	N=C	C	N=C	C	N=C
Republicans										
Increase	94.4	100.0	66.7	83.3	80.8	100.0	70.6	85.7	82.9	95.3
Decrease	0.0	0.0	22.2	0.0	3.8	0.0	0.0	0.0	3.4	0.0
Remain the same	5.5	0.0	11.1	16.7	15.4	0.0	29.4	14.3	13.6	4.6
N =	36	33	9	6	26	11	17	14	88	64
Democrats										
Increase	97.8	96.5	82.1	88.9	87.8	33.3	85.0	93.3	90.6	88.9
Decrease	0.0	1.7	5.4	0.0	3.0	22.2	0.0	0.0	1.9	1.7
Remain the same	2.1	1.7	12.5	11.1	9.0	44.4	15.0	6.7	7.3	9.3
N =	94	58	56	90	33	9	20	15	203	172
Percentage who favor a tax increase for education:										
Republicans	85.7	87.0	77.8	40.0	60.0	55.6	6.3	35.7	62.3	66.1
N =	35	31	9	5	25	31	16	15	85	59
Democrats	70.4	73.2	48.0	60.6	25.0	74.1	30.0	46.7	56.6	65.5
N =	88	56	52	89	8	31	20	15	168	191

Table 4–20 indicates that legislators from noncompetitive districts are slightly more liberal on our two educational issues than those from competitive districts. In contrast, when in Table 4–21 we compare the legislators' scores on our three attitudinal indices, we find that their attitudes on the educational issues index are not importantly differentiated according to the competitiveness of the district. Overall, legislators from competitive districts are more likely to be friendly toward education lobbyists than those from noncompetitive districts. This disposition is particularly strong among the legislators in Utah (*gamma* = .48, Sign. = .009) and North Carolina (*gamma* = .22, Sign. = .02). Surprisingly, in view of earlier findings, of the four groups the Utah delegation is most supportive of education lobbyists. At the other end of the spectrum, Massachusetts legislators react negatively to education lobbyists (*gamma* = —.10, NS), particularly those from competitive districts. Lastly, the scores on the legislative process scale indicate that legislators from competitive districts are slightly more supportive of lobbyists in general than those from noncompetitive districts. However, these figures are somewhat misleading in that North Carolina is the only state of the four where legislators from competitive districts score higher on the scale in ordinal terms (*gamma* = .23, Sign. = .02) than those from noncompetitive districts.

Political Compatibility of the District

A legislator is "compatible" with his district insofar as his party affiliation reflects his district's prior voting habits or registration preference; in other words, candidates elected from districts controlled by the opposite political party are in some sense "incompatible" with the district.

While political variables are usually associated with low scores on the education lobbyist index, we find in Table 4–22 an important exception to this pattern: legislators from incompatible districts are

---

tion because its preferences were regarded as too marginal. For a full rationale, see Michael Baer, "Environmental Effects on State Legislators and Lobbyists," Ph.D. dissertation, University of Oregon, 1968, pp. 133–35.

Table 4-21   Comparison of Legislators from Competitive and
              Noncompetitive Districts on Attitudinal Indices

		Members from Competitive Districts (N = 131)	Members from Non-competitive Districts (N = 241)
Educational Issues Index			
	High	30.5%	29.9%
x^2 = .528, Sign. = NS	Medium	40.5	41.5
gamma = +.003, Sign. = NS	Low	29.0	28.6
Education Lobbyist Index			
x^2 = 2.069, Sign. = NS	High	58.4%	51.9%
gamma = .139, Sign. = .01	Low	41.6	48.1
Legislative Process Scale			
x^2 = .129, Sign. = NS	High	35.5%	33.6%
gamma = .049, Sign. = NS	Low	64.5	66.4

highly supportive of education lobbyists. In Utah legislators from both competitive districts and incompatible districts show particular support for education lobbyists (sensing their precarious position, perhaps they are deliberately seeking support from interest groups such as education).

Compatibility and incompatibility certainly warrant more attention than they have received in past research efforts. Party competition and political compatibility are mutually dependent on the location and the population of a district. For instance, if a high proportion of the population is registered to vote and consistently turns out at the polls, the incumbent legislator will probably be more receptive to, and heedful of, his constituents' demands than one who could depend on a poor turnout almost exclusively from his own party. Further, if the legislator's supporters are concentrated in an area lacking in public services and amenities, he is likely to view policy issues quite differently from a legislator representing a safe district.

Table 4–22   Comparison of Legislators from Compatible and
Incompatible Districts on Attitudinal Indices

		Members from Compatible Districts (N = 264)	Members from Incompatible Districts (N = 143)
Educational Issues Index			
	High	30.7%	27.3%
x^2 = .835, Sign. = NS	Medium	41.7	41.3
gamma = .078, Sign. = NS	Low	27.2	31.5
Education Lobbyist Index			
x^2 = 11.167, Sign. = .001	High	53.8%	71.3%
gamma = −.363, Sign. = .001	Low	46.2	28.7
Legislative Process Scale			
x^2 = .007, Sign. = NS	High	34.8%	35.0%
gamma = −.003, Sign. = NS	Low	65.2	65.0

Urbanization

We may view urbanization from two perspectives. On the one hand, it is a component of industrialization (hence, it is positively associated with a high level of educational expenditures); on the other hand, it is a characteristic of a particular district within a state (hence, it can be examined as a variable interacting with other variables). When political scientists adopt the latter perspective, they generally discuss urbanization in the context of legislative conflict. David R. Derge has rejected the urban-rural dichotomy as providing a clear means of differentiating legislators on roll-call votes.[32] Heinz Eulau, on the other hand, found that the ecological structure is significant in Ohio

[32] David R. Derge, "Metropolitan and Outstate Alignments in Illinois and Missouri Legislative Delegations," *American Political Science Review* 41 (December 1958): 1051–65.

for urban-rural and competitive and semicompetitive districts.[33] Frank J. Sorauf has suggested that the effects of urbanization may be negated by strong Democratic-Republican splits.[34] For LeRoy Ferguson, too, the urban-rural dimension presented an interesting mixture in his four states; over 50 percent of the legislators he interviewed cited the urban-rural (cities vs. rural counties) distinction as a significant dimension for differentiating legislators on the issue of school needs (unfavorable attitudes toward education emanating primarily from the rural group).[35] It seems appropriate, then, to ask whether urbanization plays an important part in forming legislators' attitudes toward education in Massachusetts, North Carolina, Oregon, and Utah. We would hypothesize that legislators representing highly urbanized districts (which generally manifest the greatest needs for increased tax revenues for education) will favor greater educational expenditures while at the same time opposing tax increases.

Why do we state the hypothesis in this way? It seems reasonable to suggest that when educational funds are allocated on a per pupil basis, the more urbanized an area becomes, the more needs it accrues and the more money it desires. However, probably few legislators would risk their political careers by advocating that their constituents bear the increased financial burden.

The linking of urbanization, competition, and party factors should enable us to evaluate some of the past explorations into legislative behavior with specific reference to our four states. We classify the degree of urbanization as low (39 percent or less urban population in district), medium (40–59), or high (60 percent or more).

In Table 4–23 we consider legislators' attitudes toward two important educational issues, controlling for party and for the district's degree of urbanization. While the urbanization categories do not clearly differentiate attitudes toward greater expenditures for education, a different pattern emerges when we look at the question of increased taxes. Legislators from the highly urbanized districts tend to favor a tax increase for education while those from the more

[33] Heinz Eulau, "The Ecological Basis of Party Systems: The Case of Ohio," *Midwest Journal of Political Science* 1 (August 1957): 135.

[34] Sorauf, *Party and Representation*, p. 145.

[35] Ferguson, *How Legislators View School Needs*, pp. 34–37.

Table 4-23 Comparison of Legislators on Two Educational Issues According to Degree of Urbanization (High, Medium, or Low) in Member's District

Percentage who believe the proportion of expenditures for education will:

Republicans

	Mass.			*N.C.*					*Total*	
	High	Med.	Low	High	Med.	Low		High	Med.	Low
Increase	97.0	—	100.0	0.0	—	78.5		91.5	79.1	85.8
Decrease	0.0	—	0.0	100.0	—	7.1		2.1	0.0	2.0
Remain the same	2.9	—	0.0	0.0	—	14.2		6.4	20.9	12.2
N =	68	0	6	1	0	14		94	24	49

	Oreg.			*Utah*		
	High	Med.	Low	High	Med.	Low
Increase	90.0	83.4	91.7	73.4	66.7	82.4
Decrease	10.0	0.0	0.0	0.0	0.0	0.0
Remain the same	0.0	16.6	8.3	26.6	33.3	17.6
N =	10	18	12	15	6	17

Democrats

	Mass.			*N.C.*		
	High	Med.	Low	High	Med.	Low
Increase	97.9	100.0	92.3	81.4	92.5	86.3
Decrease	.6	0.0	0.0	7.4	0.0	1.0
Remain the same	1.4	0.0	7.6	11.1	7.4	12.6
N =	149	1	13	27	27	95

Table 4–23 (*continued*)

	Oreg. High	Oreg. Med.	Oreg. Low	Utah High	Utah Med.	Utah Low	Total High	Total Med.	Total Low
Increase	85.0	90.0	53.9	90.9	83.3	66.7	94.1	90.9	80.9
Decrease	5.0	0.0	15.3	4.5	0.0	0.0	2.2	0.0	2.1
Remain the same	10.0	10.0	30.8	4.5	16.6	33.3	3.6	9.0	16.9
N =	20	10	13	22	6	21	218	44	142

Percentage who favor a tax increase for education:

Republicans

	Mass. High	Mass. Med.	Mass. Low	N.C. High	N.C. Med.	N.C. Low
Republicans	86.1	100.0	83.3	100.0	—	61.6
N =	65	1	6	1	0	13

	Oreg. High	Oreg. Med.	Oreg. Low	Utah High	Utah Med.	Utah Low	Total High	Total Med.	Total Low
	60.0	55.5	44.4	13.3	40.0	18.7	73.5	54.1	45.4
N =	10	18	9	15	5	16	98	24	44

Democrats

	Mass. High	Mass. Med.	Mass. Low	N.C. High	N.C. Med.	N.C. Low
Democrats	72.4	—	66.7	64.0	52.0	56.4
N =	141	0	12	25	25	94

	Oreg. High	Oreg. Med.	Oreg. Low	Utah High	Utah Med.	Utah Low	Total High	Total Med.	Total Low
	76.9	50.0	50.0	47.6	33.3	23.8	69.0	48.7	51.7
N =	13	10	12	21	6	21	200	41	139

rural districts generally oppose an increase. At each level of urbanization the strongest opposition comes from Utah legislators. Overall, these distinctions are true for both Democrats and Republicans.

Eulau and Sorauf both believe that the urban-rural distinction may be as important as party competition in explaining differences in legislators' attitudes toward public issues. Earlier we hypothesized that legislators from highly urbanized districts, while realizing the need for greater educational expenditures, would nonetheless resist a tax increase for reasons of political expediency. The results, happily, fail to confirm this expectation: the legislators from urban districts overwhelmingly favored a tax increase for education. The levels of urbanization, however, proved useless in differentiating legislators on the three attitudinal indices. Even so, our findings agree with those of Ferguson, who concluded that urban legislators are, on the whole, more favorable toward educational interests than rural legislators.[36] Both party competition and urbanization must be studied across a broader range of regions and states if we are to enhance their explanatory power.

Membership in Senate vs. Membership in Lower House

Another structural variable related to a legislator's attitudes concerns the chamber in which he serves. Upon examination, however, we find that house membership has little explanatory value (see Table 4–24). Only with regard to the education lobbyist index does any significant trend emerge: state senators appear to be more friendly to education lobbyists than state representatives.

To this point we have found leadership status, party competition, and to a lesser extent the index of incompatibility to be consistently useful variables. We will now discuss a final structural variable, namely, interaction rates between legislators and lobbyists.

Legislator-Lobbyist Interaction Rates

In Table 4–25 the legislator's interaction rate (high or low) has been determined by breaking the range at the ordinal category that includes

[36] *Ibid.*, pp. 57–58.

Table 4–24 Comparison of State Senators and Representatives
on Attitudinal Indices

		State Senators (N = 134)	State Representatives (N = 445)
Educational Issues Index			
	High	30.6%	29.0%
x^2 = .23, Sign. = NS	Medium	41.0	40.7
gamma = −.27, Sign. = .001	Low	28.4	30.3
Education Lobbyist Index			
x^2 = 4.94, Sign. = .03	High	64.2%	52.8%
gamma = .23, Sign. = .01	Low	35.8	47.2
Legislative Process Scale			
x^2 = .44, Sign. = NS	High	30.6%	34.2%
gamma = −.08, Sign. = NS	Low	69.4	65.8

the mean for each particular state.[37] Legislators whose rate of interaction with lobbyists is high on the whole score higher on the educational issues and education lobbyist indices and lower on the legislative
process scale than those with low interaction rates. Nevertheless, each
delegation appears to have its own idiosyncracies. Oregon legislators
are least favorable on legislative process items (*gamma* = −.40, Sign.
= .04), while Massachusetts legislators are most favorable toward
the education lobbyist items (*gamma* = .40, Sign. = .01). Like our
other measures, interaction rates exhibit general trends though failing
to be consistent among the individual states.

Earlier we saw that in the direct interaction process business
interests have a strong advantage in that their representatives, constituting the largest single bloc of lobbyists and including a disproportionate number of ex-legislators, receive more solicitations from

[37] The dividing point was 10 interactions per week in Massachusetts, 10 in
North Carolina, 25 in Utah, and 51 in Oregon. See Zeigler and Baer, *Lobbying,* pp. 146–51.

Table 4–25   Comparison of Legislators Exhibiting High vs. Low Rates
of Interaction with Lobbyists on Attitudinal Indices

| | | Members' Rate of Interaction with Lobbyists | |
		High (N = 112)	Low (N = 470)
Educational Issues Index			
	High	34.8%	27.9%
x^2 = 3.04, Sign. = NS	Medium	33.9	42.1
gamma = .06, Sign. = NS	Low	31.3	30.0
Education Lobbyist Index			
x^2 = 5.95, Sign. = .01	High	66.1%	52.8%
gamma = .27, Sign. = .001	Low	33.9	47.2
Legislative Process Scale			
x^2 = 1.69, Sign. = NS	High	27.7%	34.7%
gamma = −.16, Sign. = .01	Low	72.3	65.3

legislators in response to initiated interactions than other lobbyists.[38]
We found also that the legislators who are most favorable to education lobbyists tend to hold leadership positions, to be from competitive
districts, to have a high rate of interaction with lobbyists, and to be
state senators as opposed to representatives.

Having completed our examination of the important structural
variables that appeared earlier in our regression equations, let us now
turn our attention to the absolute items, that is, to the demographic
variables.

Ferguson on Age, Educational Background, Income, and Occupation

In his study of legislators in four states LeRoy Ferguson found that
age, educational background, and occupation (but not income) were

[38] These findings support the suggestion for educational coalitions made by
Michael D. Usdan, "The Role and Future of State Educational Coalitions,"
Educational Administration Quarterly 5 (Spring 1969), 26–42.

variables helpful in explaining educational attitudes.[39] Ferguson was surprised to find that in only one of the four states (New Jersey) were legislators under 45 years of age more liberal in their attitudes toward education than the older legislators. He had expected that the younger members, many having children of their own in school, would be more favorable toward educational needs than the older members of the legislature.[40]

This expectation was not unreasonable. How do we explain the discrepancy? From another source we learn that younger legislators are disproportionately from competitive districts,[41] thus bringing a cross-pressure to bear. Age, then, might well be an important variable whose effects are disguised by intervening variables. If we can demonstrate that competitiveness of district and the legislator's own educational background (considered as the next variable) are both important variables affecting educational attitudes, then we may be able to gauge the amount of cross-pressure in the legislature by using age as the third variable. For the moment, however, Ferguson's study suggests this hypothesis: the older the legislator, the more likely he is to approve educational expenditures and additional taxes for education.

Even if the legislator's age proves to be an unimportant variable, his educational background may still help to differentiate his educational attitudes. A college education, noted Ferguson, does not necessarily lead to a more liberal attitude toward education. In fact, he concluded that legislators with college degrees tended to be *less* favorable to educational needs than those without them[42] (a finding that suggests that one way to increase educational expenditures and taxes to support education might be to elect lesser-educated persons to the legislature!).

Ferguson was unable to document a relationship between legislators' income levels and their educational attitudes. Commonly it is assumed that wealth and political conservatism go hand in hand, and we too would expect that *a legislator's income will be positively related to a conservative stance on educational expenditures and taxes.*

---

[39] Ferguson, *How Legislators View School Needs*, pp. 66 and 67.

[40] *Ibid.,* p. 54.

[41] Jewell and Patterson, *The Legislative Process*, p. 114.

[42] Ferguson, *How Legislators View School Needs*, p. 55.

If age, educational background, and income fail to provide sufficient explanation of the variations in legislators' educational attitudes, we might also investigate occupation as a fourth variable. Ferguson finds no clear pattern with respect to occupation, although he regards it as a differentiating factor.[43] Lawyers, concludes another researcher, are neither the most liberal nor the most conservative of state legislators.[44] We would expect that former teachers, having dealt first-hand with educational problems, will be the occupational group most favorable toward educational expenditures and taxes within the legislature.

The reader will note that the four variables we have chosen—age, educational background, income, and occupation—relate directly to the legislators as individual personalities. Obviously, we could have explored other variables at greater length (e.g., legislators' perceptions of the various interest groups, lobbyists' influence on legislators' opinions, legislators' sources of information); but the four we have chosen, while not exhausting the range of possibilities, certainly do allow us to compare major accessible commonalities among legislative members and the state population as a whole.

Age

Dividing age into three categories, we find in Table 4–26 that Massachusetts legislators and (to a lesser extent) Oregon legislators are disproportionately young. The high proportion of young legislators in Massachusetts might be explained by the long annual sessions and the relatively high salaries accorded members of the state's General Court (as the legislature is called). Oregon's younger legislators are concentrated predominantly in the 45–64 year bracket, leading one to believe that the state's less demanding biennial session, while less rewarding financially, attracts middle-aged types (primarily businessmen and semiretired farmers) who are most interested in the status attached to the job. In comparison with the first two states North

[43] *Ibid.,* pp. 55–57.

[44] See Charles S. Hyneman, "Who Makes Our Laws?" *Political Science Quarterly* 55 (1940): 578–80.

Table 4–26   Age Distribution of Legislators
and General Population, by State

| Percentage who are: | (*Figures for general population in parentheses*) | | | |
	Massachusetts	North Carolina	Oregon	Utah
21-44	51.4 (48.2)	33.1 (56.3)	39.3 (48.0)	25.3 (56.8)
45-64	46.0 (34.2)	54.6 (31.5)	51.2 (34.9)	57.5 (30.3)
65+	2.4 (17.6)	12.2 (12.2)	9.5 (17.1)	17.2 (12.8)
N = (in thousands)	241 (3245)	163 (2557)	84 (1073)	87 (468)

SOURCE: U.S. Bureau of the Census, *Statistical Abstract of the United States: 1966*, 88th ed. (Washington, D.C.: Government Printing Office, 1966), p. 23.

Carolina and Utah have a higher percentage of elder citizens in their legislatures.

Turning now to a comparison of educational attitudes as delineated by our three indices, we find in Table 4–27 that the older legislators (those 45 years of age and over) are not particularly favorable toward educational issues (*gamma* = —.098, Sign. = NS). Upon closer examination (figures not shown), we find that the youngest legislators (those 21–44 years old) are more favorable toward a tax increase for education (*gamma* = .105, Sign. = .02) but are less likely to anticipate an increase in educational expenditures (*gamma* = —.318, Sign. = .02) than the other two groups. Also, the younger legislators are generally more hostile toward education lobbyists and lobbyists in general than the eldest group of legislators.

Educational Background

Table 4–28 compares the educational levels of the state legislators with those of all persons over twenty-five years of age in each of the four states. Only in Utah do high school graduates constitute a majority of the population over twenty-five while in all four states a majority of legislators have college degrees. Thus, receipt of a high school diploma seems to be a convenient point for dividing the general public, whereas receipt of a college degree better subdivides the legislators.

Table 4–27   Comparison of Legislators' Scores
on Attitudinal Indices, by Age Group

		Age Group		
		21-44 (N = 235)	45-64 (N = 295)	65+ (N = 52)
Educational Issues Index				
	High	6.4%	6.8%	7.7%
x^2 = .781, Sign. = NS	Medium	43.4	38.0	38.5
gamma = +.050, Sign. = NS	Low	50.2	55.3	53.8
Education Lobbyist Index				
x^2 = .656, Sign. = NS	High	27.7%	25.8%	30.8%
gamma = +.004, Sign. = NS	Low	72.3	74.2	69.2
Legislative Process Scale				
x^2 = 1.751, Sign. = NS	High	31.1%	33.9%	40.4%
gamma = −.095, Sign. = .04	Low	68.9	66.1	59.6

Why should the completion of college make an important differ-
ence in the way legislators think? At the risk of running slightly afield,
let us suggest two possibilities. First, a college degree ceremonially
confers upon its recipient a sense of adequacy that leads to certain
role expectations. When a person acquires the sheet of paper declaring
him eligible for all rights and privileges connected with the degree, he
implicitly assumes certain responsibilities to protect the value of his
degree. Unlike the man who completes three and one-half years of
college only to quit in the final term, the degree holder is—by all
definitions that matter—an "educated man." Second, receipt of a
college degree usually indicates that one intends to pursue his studies
even further—toward a graduate or a professional degree. Of the
legislators in our sample, about 55 percent or more of the college
graduates in each of our states went on to higher schooling.

In Table 4–29 we find that the legislators' educational background does not significantly influence their expectations of increases
in educational expenditures. Among the Democrats, however, legislators with a college education are generally more inclined to antici-

Table 4–28   Cumulative Education of Legislators
             and General Population, by State

Percentage who have completed:	(*Figures for statewide population over 25 in parentheses*)			
	Massachusetts	North Carolina	Oregon	Utah
High school	98.0 (47.0)	96.4 (32.3)	97.6 (48.4)	93.3 (55.8)
Some college	70.4 (18.2)	87.2 (13.4)	78.0 (19.7)	78.6 (25.2)
College	56.0 (8.8)	64.0 (6.3)	54.8 (8.5)	57.3 (10.2)

SOURCE: Figures for general population were taken from U.S. Bureau of the Census, *U.S. Census of Population: Vol. 1, Characteristics of the Population* (Washington, D.C.: Government Printing Office, 1960), Part I, United States Summary.

pate greater educational outlays than those without a college degree in Massachusetts, Oregon, and Utah. Moreover, the better-educated Democrats in all four states favor a tax increase for education in greater proportions than the lesser-educated ones.

The Republican legislators are less clearly differentiated according to educational background. In all four states except Massachusetts, however, the better-educated Republicans disproportionately favor a tax increase for education. There appears to be no set pattern that would enable us to differentiate between the two parties on these two questions. Among legislators with college backgrounds, Republicans are more favorable toward a tax increase for education in Massachusetts and North Carolina and Democrats more favorable in Oregon and Utah. Overall, however, educational achievement does differentiate in favor of legislators' willingness to increase taxes for education (*gamma* = .178, Sign. = .001).

The legislator's educational background has greater implications in relation to our three attitudinal indices. In Table 4–30 we see that legislators who finished college score highest of the three groups on the educational issues and education lobbyist indices and second highest on the legislative process scale. Upon examining the states individually, we find that this group's positive attitudes toward educational issues are particularly strong in Oregon (*gamma* = .308, Sign. = .008) and Utah (*gamma* = .447, Sign. = .001). Similarly, the

Table 4–29 Comparison of College Graduates and Non-College Graduates on Two Educational Issues

Percentage who believe the proportion of expenditures for education will:	Mass.		N.C.		Oreg.		Utah		Total	
	C	N-C	C	N-C	C	N-C	C	N-C	C	N-C
Republicans										
Increase	97.7	96.6	71.4	75.0	83.4	93.8	80.0	69.2	88.0	88.0
Decrease	0.0	0.0	14.3	12.5	4.1	0.0	0.0	0.0	2.0	1.5
Remain the same	2.2	3.3	14.3	12.5	12.5	6.2	20.0	30.8	10.0	10.4
N =	44	30	7	8	24	16	25	13	100	67
Democrats										
Increase	100.0	94.7	84.7	90.1	93.6	66.6	88.0	75.0	90.8	87.2
Decrease	0.0	1.3	3.1	0.0	4.5	9.6	0.0	0.0	1.8	1.8
Remain the same	0.0	3.9	12.2	9.8	1.9	23.8	12.0	25.0	7.3	11.0
N =	87	76	98	51	22	21	25	24	232	172
Percentage who favor a tax increase for education:										
Republicans	85.3	86.6	71.4	57.1	69.5	28.5	21.8	15.3	64.9	56.2
N =	41	30	7	7	23	14	23	13	94	64
Democrats	75.7	68.0	59.4	52.0	76.1	52.6	56.0	12.5	66.5	53.3
N =	82	72	96	48	21	19	25	24	224	163

Table 4–30   Comparison of Legislators on Attitudinal Indices According
to Level of Educational Achievement

		Some	High
	College+ (N = 337)	College (N = 146)	School (N = 95)
Educational Issues Index			
High	7.7%	5.5%	4.2%
x^2 = 3.148, Sign. = NS Medium	41.8	37.7	40.0
gamma = .106, Sign. = .04 Low	50.4	56.8	55.8
Education Lobbyist Index			
x^2 = 7.441, Sign. = .02 High	31.2%	19.9%	23.2%
gamma = .210, Sign. = .001 Low	68.8	80.1	76.8
Legislative Process Scale			
x^2 = .850, Sign. = NS High	32.3%	36.3%	31.6%
gamma = −.025, Sign. = NS Low	67.7	63.7	68.4

college-educated legislators scored highest on the education lobbyist
index only in North Carolina (*gamma* = .347, Sign. = .001).

Income

The researcher's choice of income categories is important in determining the results of comparisons. As Table 4–31 indicates, legislators'
income levels are generally much higher than those of the general
population. Their median family incomes are almost twice as much as
the state median in Utah, more than twice the median in Massachusetts and Oregon, and almost five times the median in North
Carolina. Comparing the two highest income brackets (encompassing
all those with more than $15,000 annual family income), we see that
the greatest disproportion between legislators and the general population is in North Carolina and Oregon, although neither Utah nor
Massachusetts lags very far behind. While the best dividing point for
the general population would be at the $10,000—or perhaps even the
$5,000—level, that for the legislators would be around $15,000.

Table 4–31   Comparison of Median Family Income and Income
             Distributions for Legislators and General Population

| | (*Figures for general population in parentheses*) | | | |
	Massa-chusetts	*North Carolina*	*Oregon*	*Utah*
Median Family Income	$13,048 ($6,272)	$18,545 ($3,956)	$13,755 ($5,892)	$10,214 ($5,899)
Distribution of family incomes (in percentage):				
$25,000 +	15.7 (1.4)	32.3 (.7)	26.2 (1.2)	11.5 (.9)
$15,000-$24,999	28.9 (3.8)	32.9 (1.5)	25.0 (2.8)	13.8 (2.6)
$10,000-$14,999	29.3 (11.8)	11.6 (4.7)	33.3 (19.9)	26.4 (10.3)
$ 5,000-$ 9,999	25.6 (50.7)	20.7 (30.6)	13.1 (48.0)	36.8 (50.5)
$ 4,999 −	.4 (24.1)	2.4 (62.3)	2.4 (37.3)	11.5 (36.1)

SOURCES: U.S. Bureau of the Census, *Statistical Abstract of the United States: 1967*, 88th ed. (Washington, D.C.: Government Printing Office, 1967), p. 335; idem, *Census of the Population, 1960: The Eighteenth Decennial Census of the United States* (Washington, D.C.: Government Printing Office, 1963), pt. 23, Table 65, p. 145; pt. 35, Table 65, p. 182; pt. 38, Table 65, p. 107; and pt. 46, Table 65, p. 87.

Moreover, we must consider whether the legislator earning $15,000 annually would be likely to have the same attitudinal structure as one earning $25,000 a year.

In Table 4–32 we have divided the legislators into three income categories: $14,999 or less, $15,000-$24,999, and $25,000 or more. The table indicates that the higher their income levels, the more the legislators tend to be favorable toward both educational issues and education lobbyists. This pattern is not confined to one particular state but rather is present in all four generally on the educational issues index. On the education lobbyist index the relationship between a legislator's score and his income level is particularly strong in Oregon (*gamma* = .355, Sign. = .01). On the legislative process scale the positive associations between the scores and the legislators' incomes in North Carolina and Oregon overbalance the negative results in Utah and Massachusetts.

Table 4–32   Comparison of Legislators on Attitudinal Indices
              According to Income Level

		$25,000+ (N = 89)	$15,000-$24,999 (N = 158)	$14,999- (N = 299)
Educational Issues Index				
	High	10.1%	8.2%	5.0%
x^2 = 8.916, Sign. = .06	Medium	8.2	44.9	37.1
gamma = .198, Sign. = .001	Low	5.0	46.8	57.9
Education Lobbyist Index				
x^2 = 6.700, Sign. = .04	High	34.8%	31.6%	23.1%
gamma = .210, Sign. = .001	Low	65.2	68.4	76.9
Legislative Process Scale				
x^2 = .971, Sign. = NS	High	37.1%	31.6%	31.8%
gamma = .054, Sign. = NS	Low	62.9	68.4	68.2

Occupation

We selected occupations for our four-state analysis with three criteria
in mind: (1) the occupation's practitioners had to comprise more
than 10 percent of the legislative membership in at least one state; (2)
the occupation had to be represented in at least three of the four
states; and (3) the occupation had to be related to matters of concern
to us in this study. Thus, we included public school teachers with the
third criterion primarily in mind while excluding self-employed com-
mercial businessmen even though they satisfied the first two criteria.
In Table 4–33 we have listed the occupational groups that satisfy our
criteria along with the percentage that each comprises of the various
legislative delegations.

   Most of the occupations listed are somewhat more prestigious
callings than would be found among a typical sample of the general
population. Lawyers, judges, and businessmen generally predominate
in the legislatures' membership; moreover, one may feel certain that

Table 4–33   Occupations of Legislators, by State

	Mass. (N = 244)	N.C. (N = 164)	Oreg. (N = 84)	Utah (N = 90)
Jurists: Lawyers and Judges	25.8%	36.6%	23.8%	8.9%
Public School Teachers	2.9	1.8	3.6	11.1
Businessmen: Managers, Officials, and Proprietors	15.2	22.0	17.9	14.4
Businessmen: Salesmen	15.2	2.4	10.7	7.8
Farmers	0.0	12.8	10.7	14.4

the salesmen in the legislature are not of the door-to-door variety, nor the farmers of the mule-and-plow type.

Since the Massachusetts legislature is in session almost full-time, it includes very few teachers or farmers. State legislatures that meet for only a short period every two years enable most legislators to maintain their regular occupations with a minimum of inconvenience. Since the North Carolina and Oregon legislatures are characterized by short sessions and adequate compensation, we would expect them to attract more farmers and public school teachers than the Massachusetts General Court. Our results partially confirm this expectation: only a few of the legislators in these two states are teachers, but more than 10 percent are farmers. In Utah, also characterized by short legislative sessions, the results are more gratifying: teachers and farmers there constitute fully one-quarter of the legislative membership.

Earlier in this chapter we speculated that teachers would probably be most favorable to educational interests. Comparing the scores on our three attitudinal indices, we find in Table 4–34 that 11.6 percent of the farmers score high on the educational issues index as compared to smaller percentages of, respectively, teachers, businessmen, and jurists (i.e., lawyers and judges). Furthermore, a highly disproportionate number of farmers (69.8 percent), as compared to the other groups, have low scores on the index. Therefore, combining the medium- and high-score distributions, we conclude that jurists tend to be most favorable toward educational issues, followed respectively by teachers, businessmen, and farmers. Overall, teacher-legislators score highest on the education lobbyist index and third highest on the

Table 4–34   Comparison of Legislators on Attitudinal Indices
             According to Occupation

		Jurists (N = 151)	Teachers (N = 23)	Business-men (N = 136)	Farmers (N = 43)
Educational Issues Index					
	High	7.9%	8.7%	8.0%	11.6%
	Medium	45.0	43.5	38.2	18.6
	Low	47.0	47.8	53.6	69.8
Education Lobbyist Index					
	High	34.4%	39.1%	23.5%	30.2%
	Low	65.6	60.9	76.5	69.8
Legislative Process Scale					
	High	33.1%	26.1%	31.6%	23.3%
	Low	66.9	73.9	68.4	76.7

legislative process scale, although the response patterns vary tremendously according to state.

Having completed our analysis of the four demographic variables, let us next consider the extent to which legislators' scores on the three attitudinal indices are indicative of their responses to our two questions regarding educational expenditures and taxes. In Table 4–35 we have divided the legislators according to their scores on the three indices and their answers to the two questions. We find, first, that a legislator's score on the educational issues index does not importantly indicate whether or not he anticipates greater expenditures for education; however, a high score does indicate a favorability toward a tax increase for education. These findings denote a sense of pessimism on the part of legislators supporting education; that is, although the legislators scoring high on the educational issues index favor educational progress in their respective states, they are no more optimistic than those scoring low on the index regarding increased allotments to education. This undertone of pessimism is probably greatest in North Carolina (*gamma* = —.215, Sign. = .05) and

Table 4–35 Comparison of Legislators' Scores on Attitudinal Indices and Responses on Two Educational Issues

		Educational Issues Index			Education Lobbyist Index		Legislative Process Scale	
		High	Med.	Low	High	Low	High	Low
Percentage who believe the proportion of expenditures for education will:	(N)							
Increase	(512)	87.0	86.0	95.3	86.8	91.8	86.8	90.9
Remain the same	(53)	11.8	13.1	1.2	11.3	6.6	11.6	8.1
Decrease	(10)	1.2	.8	3.5	1.9	1.6	1.6	1.8
N =		169	236	170	319	256	190	385
		gamma = −.254 Sign. = .001			gamma = −.251 Sign. = .04		gamma = −.154 Sign. = NS	
Percentage who favor or oppose a tax increase for education:	(N)							
Favor	(336)	96.5	69.3	10.4	59.3	63.5	63.6	60.1
Oppose	(213)	3.5	30.7	89.6	40.7	36.5	36.4	39.9
N =		170	225	154	305	244	176	373
		gamma = .926 Sign. = .001			gamma = −.088 Sign. = NS		gamma = .076 Sign. = NS	

Utah (*gamma* = —.738, Sign. = .001). Overall, however, state legislators strongly support a tax increase for education (*gamma* = .926, Sign. = .001).

A friendly attitude toward education lobbyists (as indicated by a high score on the education lobbyist index) does not necessarily denote an optimistic view about future educational allotments in any of the states. Similarly, a legislator's attitudes toward lobbyists in general (as measured by the legislative process scale) bear only slightly on his expectation of budgetary increases for education.

Although the states' share of educational expenditures is actually decreasing—a point we made earlier—the great majority of legislators believe that education will get a greater share of the state budgets of the future. Lastly, let us add the observation that legislators who score high on the educational issues index disproportionately favor a tax increase to support education.

We will now close our circle of inquiry by examining contextual variations in relation to our attitudinal measures.

Attitudinal Indices and Responses in Relation to Contextual Variables

Earlier, in Chapter 3, we found that our four states are well distributed in the rankings of the fifty states on the progressive liberalism and federalism-and-concern factors. In Table 4–36 we have listed the states according to the rank of their factor scores in order to compare on a contextual basis their legislators' scores on the three attitudinal indices and their responses to our two specific questions.

Massachusetts was highest of our four states on the progressive liberalism factor—a strongly political measure—and lowest on the federalism-and-concern factor. The distributions for the three indices and two responses indicate that legislators in wealthy states that in the past have traditionally supported education and that generally deal with problems of higher education in a nonpolitical manner tend to support educational issues, to anticipate increased budgetary allotments for education, and to favor additional taxes for education. Conversely, in poorer states more politically oriented, legislators tend to be friendlier to education lobbyists, slightly more pessimistic toward

Table 4-36 Comparison of States' Rankings on Factor Scores and Legislative Delegations' Scores on Attitudinal Indices and Responses on Two Educational Issues

		Ranking on Progressive Liberalism Factor Score			
		(1st) Mass.	(11th) Oreg.	(25th) Utah	(45th) N.C.
Educational Issues Index					
	High	34.8%	26.2%	20.0%	27.4%
	Medium	38.1	47.6	25.6	48.8
	Low	27.0	26.2	54.4	23.8
x^2 = 35.793, Sign. = .001					
gamma = .079, Sign. = .02					
Education Lobbyist Index					
	High	41.4%	79.8%	78.9%	50.6%
	Low	58.6	20.2	21.1	49.4
x^2 = 61.149, Sign. = .001					
gamma = −.192, Sign. = .001					
Legislative Process Scale					
	High	33.2%	34.5%	17.8%	41.5%
	Low	66.8	65.5	82.2	58.5
	N =	244	84	90	164
x^2 = 14.734, Sign. = .002					
gamma = −.064, Sign. = NS					
Percentage who believe the proportion of expenditures for education will:					
	Increase	97.5	81.9	79.8	85.4
	Remain the same	2.1	13.3	20.2	11.6
	Decrease	.4	4.8	0.0	3.0
	N =	239	83	89	164
x^2 = 40.19, Sign. = .001					
gamma = .449, Sign. = .001					

Percentage who favor or
oppose a tax increase
for education:

| | | Ranking on Federalism-and-Concern Factor Score | | |
	(4th) Utah	(28th) N.C.	(34th) Oreg.	(45th) Mass.
Favor	76.7	59.7	28.7	57.6
Oppose	23.3	40.3	71.3	42.4
N =	227	77	87	158

$x^2 = 62.38$, Sign. = .001
gamma = .331, Sign. = .001

Educational Issues Index

	Utah	N.C.	Oreg.	Mass.
High	20.0%	27.4%	26.2%	34.8%
Medium	25.6	48.8	47.6	38.1
Low	54.4	23.8	26.2	27.0

$x^2 = 35.79$, Sign. = .001
gamma = −.18, Sign. = .001

Education Lobbyist Index

	Utah	N.C.	Oreg.	Mass.
High	78.9%	50.6%	79.8%	41.4%
Low	21.1	49.4	20.2	58.6

$x^2 = 61.149$, Sign. = .001
gamma = .331, Sign. = .001

Legislative Process Scale

	Utah	N.C.	Oreg.	Mass.
High	17.8%	41.5%	34.5%	33.2%
Low	82.2	58.5	65.5	66.8
N =	90	164	84	244

$x^2 = 14.734$, Sign. = .002
gamma = −.068, Sign. = .06

Table 4-36 (continued)

Percentage who believe the proportion of expenditures for education will:

Increase	79.8	85.4	81.9	97.5
Remain the same	20.2	11.6	13.3	2.1
Decrease	0.0	3.0	4.8	.4
N =	89	8	83	239

$x^2 = 40.92$, Sign. $= .001$
gamma $= -.466$, Sign. $= .001$

Percentage who favor or oppose a tax increase for education:

Favor	28.7	57.6	40.3	76.7
Oppose	71.3	42.4	59.7	23.3
N =	87	158	77	227

$x^2 = 62.37$, Sign. $= .001$
gamma $= -.480$, Sign. $= .001$

increased outlays for education, and hostile to tax increases. Legislators in certain states manifest mixed patterns of behavior not in conformity with these two generalizations; for example, Oregon legislators are both highly supportive of educational interests (as reflected in their high scores on the educational issues index) and of education lobbyists as well. General attitudes toward lobbyists are probably idiosyncratic to each legislature since we are unable to discern any meaningful patterns on the distributions for the legislative process scale.

Conclusions

Earlier we suggested that highly industrialized states that support education at the aggregate level would likely have in their legislatures a disproportionate number of individuals who support education on a personal basis. Our four-state analysis has confirmed this expectation. At the same time, we have found that structural variables (such as interaction rates, district competition factors, and leadership roles within the legislature) may often deflect a legislator from voting on the basis of his personal beliefs. Attitudes often bear little on voting behavior. The future pattern of budgetary increases and decreases for education may well depend on the interaction and interplay of the structural variables. Let us, then, briefly summarize our findings in this chapter.

First, our own analysis disputed LeRoy Ferguson's claim that older legislators are more favorable toward educational interests than younger ones. Admittedly, our own results were mixed. We did find that the younger legislators, though, while less likely to anticipate increased educational outlays than the older group, are disproportionately favorable toward both educational issues and a tax increase for education. A not unreasonable corollary would suggest that the age group controlling the legislature (e.g., a relatively young group in Massachusetts and a relatively old one in Utah) will probably perpetuate its attitudes for years to come by gradually instilling its values and convictions in other members.

Second, our analysis also disagreed with Ferguson's finding that lesser-educated legislators are more favorable to educational interests than college-educated ones. We found, instead, that the better-educated members scored higher on both the educational issues and education lobbyist indices than their lesser-educated colleagues. Specifically, we used the conferral of a college degree as the differentiating factor and discovered that legislators with degrees scored higher on the two indices and more consistently favored a tax increase for education than those without degrees. This finding suggests that today's well-educated legislator is scarcely ever regarded as "an egghead" and that he can function doubly to defend educational values and institutions from attack while serving in a position requiring expertise in the legislature. We would expect that as educational levels rise both within the general population and within the legislature, the legislator's educational background will become an increasingly important factor contributing to his support for education. Of course, at some future date there will have to be a leveling-off point (as suggested by Hofferbert[45]) after which education organizations will have to assert themselves all the harder to increase legislators' support of education.

Third, after noting Ferguson's conclusion that legislators' income levels and educational attitudes are not related to one another, we hypothesized somewhat intuitively that conservative attitudes on educational issues would be associated most with high levels of income. Using three income categories, we found—much to our surprise —that the legislators in the highest income bracket ($25,000 plus) scored highest on all three attitudinal indices. The question of proper pay for the legislator, if we may embark on a tangent, is connected to the question of what social product we expect from the legislature. James Nathan Miller has suggested that higher pay for members would help to attract more competent and skillful technicians and professionals, thus upgrading the quality of the state legislatures.[46] We would suggest that higher pay might also engender greater competition for the jobs and cause campaign costs to soar, thus effectively excluding all but the wealthiest or best-financed contenders from the field. More than higher salaries, legislators should be provided adequate facilities

---

[45] Hofferbert, "Ecological Development and Policy Change," p. 478.
[46] James Nathan Miller, "Hamstrung Legislatures," *National Civic Review* 54 (April 1965): 180–82.

to serve their constituents, and they should be encouraged to eliminate antiquated institutional machinery.

Fourth, after noting Ferguson's inconclusive findings regarding the importance of the legislator's occupation to his educational attitudes, we speculated that teachers would probably be the group most favorable to educational interests. Our four-state analysis disclosed that medium or high scores on the educational issues index were most common, respectively, among jurists, teachers, businessmen, and farmers. We concluded that farmers were most conservative and jurists most liberal toward educational issues; that businessmen were in general negatively disposed toward educational issues; and that teachers, while few in number (almost all of them in the Democratic party) were generally liberal toward educational issues, though not uniformly so in each state. The broader implications of these findings are worth noting. In states where teachers—and professionals generally—are well organized, the organization's ideological stance may inhibit member-legislators from expressing and acting upon their own predispositions and convictions. Of course, the extent to which occupational interest groups affect their member-legislators' views is a subject deserving greater attention and more research.

The variables that we have found most helpful in explaining educational attitudes and outcomes are the legislator's party affiliation, leadership status, the level of urbanization and party competition in his district, and his educational background. We have seen that the value of contextual variables is limited: mainly, they are useful in defining the setting in which structural and analytical variables operate. Perhaps the next step in research is to ask to what extent constituents' views explain the disparities between legislators' attitudes and their voting behavior.

Let us reemphasize at this juncture three main points:

1. Massachusetts, North Carolina, Oregon, and Utah are not only broadly representative of the fifty states generally (as evidenced by their scattered rankings on the two factor scores) but are also broadly reflective of the regional patterns in educational allocations.

2. Legislators' educational attitudes (as measured by their scores on our three attitudinal indices) are shaped primarily by idiosyn-

cratic personal factors; that is, they are only marginally affected by global and structural variables.

3. Educational voting patterns in Oregon proved reducible to four factors that related, respectively, to school board power and citizen participation, appropriations and development, school technical services, and educational concern. The voting patterns were explained only partially by structural variables and even less by analytical variables. (The reader may view the correlations among our three attitudinal indices and the four voting patterns in Table 4–37. None of the indices is highly correlated with any of the voting patterns. This lack of association was earlier indicated by the lesser positions that these attitudinal measures took in the weak regression equations for the voting patterns.)

In this chapter we have shown that attempts to relate global, structural, and analytical variables to educational attitudes and outcomes have thus far left most of the territory uncharted. Lest the reader become too discouraged by the weak linkages between attitudes and voting patterns, he would do well to keep in mind some observations by Martin Fishbein. Noting the recent appearance of numerous studies that failed to show strong correlations between beliefs (isolated statements or feelings about an object or situation), attitudes, behavioral intentions (statements about future action), and actual behavior, Fishbein observed that

> even if an individual's beliefs about an object and/or his behavioral intentions toward the object are considered, it is not likely that behavioral prediction will be improved. First, these variables may be highly correlated with traditional measures of attitudes, and thus they will not explain additional variance in behavior. Second, even if this is not the case (i.e., even if beliefs and behavioral intentions that are unrelated to attitude are selected for consideration), they may still be unrelated to the behavior. That is, viewing the attitude-behavior within the framework of a multiattitude object–multimethod approach, it becomes clear that the most important determinants of behavior may be other variables than an individual's beliefs about, attitude toward, or general intentions toward, a given object. Indeed, this approach clearly indicates that behavior toward an object may be completely determined by situational or individual difference

Table 4–37   Correlations Between Attitudinal Indices
and Educational Voting Patterns in Oregon

| | *Scores on* | | |
Scores on:	Educational Issues Index	Education Lobbyist Index	Legislative Process Scale
Factor 1: School Board Power and Citizen Participation	.020	−.041	.146
Factor 2: Appropriations and Development	−.061	−.003	.049
Factor 3: School Technical Services	.116	−.098	−.195
Factor 4: Educational Concern	−.015	.143	−.023

variables, rather than any variable associated with the stimulus object
per se. In other words, this approach points out that behavior toward
a given object is a function of many variables, of which attitude
toward the object is only one.[47]

In other words, particular circumstances and situations may be more
salient to a legislator when he casts his vote than his more generalized
—and less obtrusive—attitudinal structure. The point is that attitudes
form only one part—of the legislative process—but a part of sufficient
importance to warrant study in its own right.

[47] Martin Fishbein, "Attitude and the Prediction of Behavior," in *Readings in
Attitude Theory and Measurement,* ed. Fishbein (New York: John Wiley,
1967), p. 491.

chapter 5

Consequences: A Review of Local Studies and a Perspective on the Future

Our basic thesis throughout this study has been that educational policy outcomes are determined by the interplay of environmental factors (i.e., contextual or global variables), characteristics of the political system (i.e., structural variables), the personal characteristics of legislators (i.e., analytical or absolute variables), and the relations between them (i.e., relational variables). In this chapter we shall discuss the types of variables that are currently being used to evaluate educational activity at the local level and shall restate the broad conclusions of this study.

We have reviewed much of the current literature to determine what types of variables are being used to analyze community conflicts over educational questions, whether economic or noneconomic in nature. Let us briefly summarize the findings of these studies and speculate on future areas for research.

Analyses of Educational Conflict at the Local Level

In Table 5–1 we have outlined four major conflict areas that have been emphasized in educational research since 1960, namely, finances

Table 5–1   The Study of Educational Conflicts in Communities:
A Synopsis of the Literature

Finances and Expenditures

Bloomberg, Warren, Jr., and Sunshine, Morris, with Favaro, Thomas J. *Suburban Power Structures and Public Education: A Study of Values, Influence, and Tax Effort* (Syracuse, N.Y.: Syracuse University Press 1963).

Community: Upstate New York   *Key variables:* Citizen support in suburbia and central city

Carter, Richard F. *Voters and Their Schools* (Stanford, Calif.: Stanford University Press, 1960).

Community: 1054 school districts   *Key variables:* Attitudes, voter turnout

Dye, Thomas R. "City-Suburban Social Distance and Public Policy." *Social Forces* 44 (September 1965): 100–6.

Community: Milwaukee, Madison,   *Key variables:* Social character of district (taxation, services)
Green Bay, Racine, Kenosha,
38 suburbia communities

Gross, Neal. "Who Controls the Schools?" In *Education and Public Policy*, ed. Seymour E. Harris (Berkeley, Calif.: McCutchan Publishing Corporation, 1965), pp. 19–29.

Community: Six cities   *Key variables:* Power structures

Horton, J. E., and Thompson, W. E. "Powerlessness and Political Negativism: A Study of Defeated Local Referendums." *American Journal of Sociology* 67 (March 1962): 485–93.

Community: Upstate New York   *Key variables:* Attitudes of participants
(2 communities)   after defeat

Masotti, Louis H. *Education and Politics in Suburbia: The New Trier Experience* (Cleveland, Ohio: The Press of Western Reserve University, 1967)ʻ

Community: Chicago (New Trier   *Key variables:* Community vs. school
Township)   and political leadership

Masotti, Louis H. "Patterns of White and Nonwhite School Referenda Participation and Support: Cleveland, 1960–61." In *Educating an Urban Population*, ed. Marilyn Gittell (Beverly Hills, Calif.: Sage Publications, 1967), 240–55.

181

Table 5–1   (*continued*)

Finances and Expenditures

Community: Cleveland   *Key variables:* White-nonwhite,
                                          mixed wards

Minar, David W. "The Community Basis of Conflict in School System Politics." *American Sociological Review* 31 (December 1966): 822–34.

Community: Chicago suburbs   *Key variables:* High status of suburbs
                                          (favorable to education)

Odell, William R., *et al. Voters and Their Schools and Communities and Their
   Schools* (Stanford, Calif.: Stanford Institute for Communications Research, 1960).

Community: 1054 school districts   *Key variables:* Attitudes, community
                                          and voter characteristics, participation

Rosenthal, Alan. "The Special Case of Public Education." In *Cases in State
   and Local Government*, ed. Richard T. Frost (Englewood Cliffs, N.J.:
   Prentice-Hall, 1961), pp. 62–75.

Community: Parkside, New York   *Key variables:* Group and school
                                          leadership activity

---

Desegregation

Beker, Jerome. *A Study of Integration in Racially Imbalanced Urban Public
   Schools: Final Report* (New York: Syracuse University Youth Development Center, 1967).

Community: Centerline school   *Key variables:* Community politics
system   and an integration team

Billington, Monroe. "Public School Integration in Missouri, 1954–64."
   Journal of Negro Education 35 (Summer 1966): 252–62.

Community: St. Louis,   *Key variables:* School policy,
Kansas City, Mo.   citizen participation

Campbell, Ernest Q. *When a City Closes Its Schools* (Chapel Hill, N.C.:
   Institute for Research in Social Science, University of North Carolina,
   1960).

Community: Norfolk, Va.   *Key variables:* Attitudes of participants
                                          toward closing schools to avoid
                                          desegregation

182

Table 5-1 (*continued*)

<hr>

Desegregation

<hr>

Crain, Robert; Inger, Morton; Vanecko, James; and McWorter, Gerald. *The Politics of School Desegregation* (Chicago: Aldine, 1968).

Community: San Francisco, Miami, New Orleans, Jacksonville, Pittsburgh, Baltimore, Buffalo, Newark, Atlanta, Montgomery, Columbus (Ga.), St. Louis, Bay City, Lawndale

Key variables: Political leadership and citizen status (against acquiescence)

Dye, Thomas R. "Urban School Segregation: A Comparative Analysis." *Urban Affairs Quarterly* 4 (December 1968): 141–65.

Community: 55 cities

Key variables: Aggregate social, political, economic indicators

Inger, Morton. *Politics and Reality in an American City: The New Orleans School Crisis of 1960* (New York: Center for Urban Education, 1968).

Community: New Orleans

Key variables: Political leadership

Inger, Morton, and Stout, Robert T. "School Desegregation: The Need to Govern." *The Urban Review* 3 (November 1968): 35–38.

Community: Englewood, Berkeley, Teaneck, Syracuse, Coatesville, Rochester, Greenburgh, White Plains

Key variables: School leadership in forming public opinion

Lang, Kurt, and Lang, Gladys Engel. "Resistance to School Desegregation: A Study of Backlash among Jews." *Sociological Inquiry* 35 (Winter 1965): 94–106.

Community: New York, P.S. 149Q and P.S. 92Q

Key variables: Community support, neighborhood school concept

Luchterhand, Elmer, and Weller, Leonard. "Social Class and the Desegregation Movement: A Study of Parents' Decisions in a Negro Ghetto." *Social Problems* 13 (Summer 1965): 83–88.

Community: New Rochelle, New York

Key variables: Negro attitudes toward transfers

Noland, James R.; Robinson, Jerry, Jr.; and Martin, Edwin." How It Was in Houston, Texas." *Integrated Education* 7 (May–June 1969): 38–43.

Community: Houston

Key variables: Legal action and integration formulas

Table 5–1   (*continued*)

Desegregation

Rogers, David, and Swanson, Bert. "White Citizen Response to the Same Integration Plan: Comparisons of Local School Districts in a Northern City." *Sociological Inquiry* 35 (Winter 1956): 107–22.

Community: "Smithwood" and "Adamsville"

Key variables: Local decision participation, administrators' compliance, prior integration in the area

Swanson, Bert. *The Struggle for Equality: School Integration Controversy in New York* (New York: Hobbs, Dorman, 1966).

Community: New York

Key variables: Citizen participation, school administrators' role

---

School Policy

Dentler, Robert A. "The Controversy Over I.S. 201: One View and a Proposal." *The Urban Review* 1 (July 1966): 16–17.

Community: New York District 201

Key variables: Local interest group control (pro)

Dye, Thomas R.; Liebman, Charles S.; Williams, Oliver P.; and Herman, Harold. "Differentiation and Cooperation in a Metropolitan Area." *Midwest Journal of Political Science* 7 (May 1963): 145–55.

Community: 238 Philadelphia-area municipalities

Key variables: Social distance

Gittell, Marilyn, and Hollander, T. Edward. *Six Urban School Districts: A Comparative Study of Institutional Response* (New York: Praeger, 1968).

Community: Baltimore, Chicago, Detroit, New York, St. Louis, Philadelphia

Key variables: Fiscal status (doubts), administration, community participation

Mayer, Martin. *The New York City Teachers Strike* (New York: Harper and Row, 1969).

Community: New York

Key variables: Decentralization

Scott, Johnie. "My Home Is Watts." In *Readings on the School in Society*, ed. Patricia Cayo Sexton (Englewood Cliffs, N.J.: Prentice-Hall, 1967), pp. 136–38.

Community: Los Angeles (Watts)

Key variables: Social conditions and school role

184

Table 5-1   (*continued*)

School Policy

Sigel, Roberta, and Friesema, H. Paul. "Urban Community Leader's Knowledge of Public Opinion." *Western Political Quarterly* 18 (December
1965): 881–95.

Community: Detroit   *Key variables:* Perception of
                                       community acceptance by leadership

Smith, R. V.; Flory, Stan; Bashshur, Rashid; and Piel, Walter. *Community
Organization and Support of the Schools: A Study of Citizen Reaction
to the Birmingham, Michigan, Public Schools* (Ypsilanti, Mich.: Michigan
State University), Cooperative Research Project No. 1828, 1964.

Community: Birmingham,   *Key variables:* Social organization
Michigan

Wilcox, Preston R. "The Controversy Over I.S. 201: One View and a Proposal." *The Urban Review* 1 (July 1966): 13–16.

Community: New York   *Key variables:* School and interest
District 201   group relationships (con)

Teacher-Community Relations

Jennings, M. Kent, and Zeigler, Harmon. "The Politics of Teacher-Admin-
istrator Relations." *Education and Social Science* 1 (1969): 73–82.

Community: National sample of   *Key variables:* Support from
86 public schools   community and administrators

Rosenthal, Alan. *Pedagogues and Power: Teacher Groups in School Politics*
(Syracuse, N.Y.: Syracuse University Press, 1969).

Community: Boston, New York,   *Key variables:* Organizational conflict
San Francisco, Chicago,
Atlanta

---

and expenditures, desegregation, school policy, and teacher-com-
munity relations. Most of the works listed are case studies of particular
conflicts from which the researchers attempt to derive a generalized
formula for handling or resolving similar conflicts in the future. The
variables used to analyze these conflicts differ from one case to the
next. We are suggesting that it may now be possible to take some
exploratory steps toward unifying the approaches and methods chosen
for studying these problems.

Earlier, in Chapters 3 and 4, we used factor analysis and multiple regression techniques to summarize, order, and predict outcomes for state educational issues. We introduced economic determinants as needed, much in line with the thinking of researchers who see legislative outputs (in a general systems model) as the product of economic inputs. Recently Thomas R. Dye applied the economic model to the study of urban education.[1] Dye included several noneconomic outcomes (such as student dropout rates and teacher turnover rates) and a few political variables (relating mainly to school board selection and local governmental institutions) in his analysis, but he insisted on using only a few input variables (e.g., population size, level of adult education, occupation, income, racial composition, and value of property).[2] While apprehending a connection between economic inputs and economic outcomes, Dye goes on to stress the weakness of the relationships between economic variables and the ability to pay, the teaching environment in the schools, selection of school board members and the tax assessor, city control over the schools, and type (partisan or nonpartisan) of ballot.[3] Hence, his study indicates that a broad approach such as we advocate here is appropriate to city systems.

Certain types of outputs, such as desegregation policies, may be classified and thereby more fully delineated by using factor analysis. Variables used in the study of state outcomes are equally applicable to the study of city outcomes. Certainly, regression analysis can be appropriately used once the broad outlines have been defined. David C. Ranney has used regression analysis to study per pupil educational expenditures in the central city;[4] Terry N. Clark has used it to measure the impact of community structures, civic organizations, and governmental forms on city budgets and urban renewal;[5] and H. Thomas

[1] Thomas R. Dye, "Governmental Structure, Urban Environment, and Educational Policy," *Midwest Journal of Political Science* 11 (February 1967): 353–80.

[2] *Ibid.*, 356.

[3] *Ibid.*, 373–77.

[4] David C. Ranney, "The Impact of Metropolitanism on Central City Education," *Educational Administration Quarterly* 5 (Winter 1969): 24–36.

[5] Terry N. Clark, "Community Structures, Decision-Making, Budget Expenditures, and Urban Renewal in 51 American Communities," *American Sociological Review* 33 (August 1968): 576–93.

James and Jerry Miner have used it to predict expenditures in school districts.[6] We do not deny that economic variables are importantly related to many educational outcomes. We simply believe that regression analysis can help to calibrate the worth of each type of variable in relation to each educational outcome. We would suggest that the research on local educational systems can be improved in several ways.

1. The researcher should consider including analytical variables (e.g., average rental rates, occupational distributions, educational achievement levels, and income levels) for each community examined. He might also include sociometric rankings of the various school board members and interest group representatives involved in educational policy making, as these could prove useful in making comparisons. As contextual variables he might include measures of the power structures in the school district, ward, metropolitan area, county, and state.[7]

2. The researcher should consider using structural variables in any factor analysis he undertakes. Useful variables might include the proportion of *de facto* segregated schools in the city, the methods used to select school board members in relation to those used to select other school officials, and measures of the school board's autonomy and its accessibility to interest groups, as well as other political characteristics of the community.[8]

3. The researcher should consider utilizing wider-range variables such as state factor scores, tax resources, levels of industrialization, and regional attitudes toward education; also, he may usefully employ schemes for classifying issues or school districts according to the

[6] H. Thomas James, *Determinants of Educational Expenditures in Large Cities of the United States* (Stanford, Calif.: School of Education, Stanford University, 1966); and Jerry Miner, *Social and Economic Factors in Spending for Public Education* (Syracuse, N.Y.: Syracuse University Press, 1963).

[7] This point has been suggested to the author by John Orbell. See also Robert E. Agger, Daniel Goldrich, and Bert E. Swanson, *Rulers and the Ruled* (New York: John Wiley, 1964); and Robert Hagedorn and Sanford Labovitz, "Participation in Community Associations by Occupation: A Test of Three Theories," *American Sociological Review* 33 (April 1968): 272–83.

[8] Ernest Q. Campbell and C. Norman Alexander, "Structural Effects and Interpersonal Relationships," *American Journal of Sociology* 71 (November 1965): 284–89.

attitudinal intensity of community leaders and school board members.[9]

By using a variety of levels of analysis, we can better move through the "tunnel of causality," make more accurate predictions about conflicts and their resolution, and, hopefully, more fully appreciate the dynamics of educational policy making at the local level.

Summary

Throughout this study we have been seeking at the state level answers to the questions posed in the preceding section. By exposing existing data to a variety of conceptual models and variables, we have sought to advance the study of educational policy making in the fifty states. Let us briefly review our most important findings.

We found, first, that educational outcomes relating to finances or expenditures are largely determined by the economic indicators within a state, whereas noneconomic outcomes are more closely related to social and political variables. In either case, current allocations for most educational items are closely associated with prior allocations. More importantly, *changes* in educational expenditures are the joint product of social and political, as well as economic, variables. Hence, we concluded that our first model, the economic model, was inadequate as an explanatory schema.

To supplement our first model we introduced a second one, namely, the legislative model. We are convinced that to expand our knowledge of educational policy making maximally we must increasingly employ variables relating to power structures, elite characteristics, and intergovernmental relations. A comprehensive understanding of educational allocations must rest on a familiarity with several types of variables rather than a preoccupation with one. Among the state analytical variables that we found useful in our analysis were per capita income, state and local revenues per capita,

[9] Acquiescence, school board cohesiveness, and strength of political parties have been suggested as useful measures for the study of desegregation in the North by Robert L. Crain and Donald B. Rosenthal, "Community Status as a Dimension of Local Decision-Making," *American Sociological Review* 32 (December 1967): 970–84.

and median age of population. Structural variables that were important included the party competition index in the senate and the Democratic percentage of membership in the lower house. Among the global variables that consistently appeared in our regression equations were the urban percentage of the total population, Hofferbert's "cultural enrichment" factor, the Gini index, and the federal percentage of total welfare expenditures. Only after researchers have achieved a more balanced understanding of the various indicator levels will they be able to appreciate fully the complex dynamics of this allocation process.

Second, we found in our study of Oregon legislators that educational voting patterns were related to several types of variables. Among these were absolute variables (the legislator's age, educational background, income, and his scores on the various attitudinal indices), a relational item (rate of interaction with lobbyists), structural indicators (house vs. senate membership, legislator's percentage of vote in the latest primary and general election), and various global variables (extent of urbanization and degree of political incompatibility in the legislator's district). Legislators' attitudes are but part of the calculus that determines a voting decision; they must be constantly balanced against the other variables—global, structural, and analytical. The variety of forces impinging on a legislator—and the constant interplay among them—cannot easily be overestimated; they deserve continued and more precise study by political scientists.[10]

Third, we found that legislators' educational attitudes were not highly predictable. We were, however, able to detect a few interesting relationships. Specifically, we found that scores on the educational issues index were positively related at the ordinal level to a high level of educational achievement and a high level of income; moreover, teacher-legislators and jurists tended to score high on this index, as did rank-and-file legislators (as opposed to leaders). Scores were generally highest in states that had high progressive liberalism factor scores. Similarly, we found that scores on our second attitudinal index, the education lobbyist index, were likewise positively associated with high levels of educational achievement and income. State senators

[10] This point is emphasized by Alexander Heard, "Reform: Limits and Opportunities," in *State Legislatures in American Politics,* ed. Heard (Englewood Cliffs, N.J.: Prentice-Hall, 1966), p. 156.

tended to score higher on this index than state representatives, as did also legislative leaders (as opposed to nonleaders) and members from competitive and incompatible districts; legislators with high rates of interaction with lobbyists also scored well. Scores on this index were generally highest in states that had high scores on the federalism-and-concern factor. Lastly, high scores on our third attitudinal measure, the legislative process scale, were disproportionately common among older members of the legislature; scores were particularly high in states with high federalism-and-concern factor scores.

Insofar as we can categorize the legislators according to their attitudes, these two images emerge. The older, more politically involved legislators tend to be friendly to lobbyists in general and education lobbyists in particular but less friendly to the causes they promote, whereas the better-educated, affluent rank-and-file members (particularly those in wealthy industrialized states that have traditionally supported education) are more favorable to educational interests, if not to the lobbyists' promotional activities.

Lastly, having concentrated our analysis on only four states of the fifty, we are more than ever convinced that rigorous theory building can only take place in the presence of comprehensive data. A greater variety of states must be studied in much greater detail before we can even begin to approximate a general theory of state educational policy making.

In the meantime, let us offer three observations relevant to the politics of education, some with normative judgments implied or expressed.

1. A sizable resource capacity and a sense of commitment to education are prerequisites of liberal educational allocations. Of course, federal grants to education may enhance a state's relative capacity to support education. Yet there is no substitute for a legislature that is willing to tax its citizens sufficiently to ensure that its educational system offers each child a healthy setting for the maximum development of his talents.

2. If educational interests are to prosper, voters must increasingly elect legislators attuned to the sophisticated educational needs of a democratic society in a technological age. These legislators must be able to operate independently of any political group or interest group;

many of them, hopefully, will be former teachers or educators who can usefully bring a personal familiarity with educational problems to bear on the legislative process. Education groups would be well advised to recruit former state legislators with continuing contacts in the leglislature as their representatives in the state capital. So doing would assure the groups an advantageous source of entry into the allocation process; their lobbyists would be dealing with a clientele of friends and former associates whose trust and respect would provide them a special power-base from which to operate—either to persuade *or* to pressure. In contrast to this ideal, education lobbyists are at present rated very powerful, but they are generally ineffective in converting their views into legislation.

3. Citizens who genuinely support education should constantly study their state representatives' voting records to determine whether the legislators' actions on education bills conform to their campaign rhetoric on educational needs. Votes, not attitudes, allocate the resources.

Furthermore, we would suggest that in the future researchers studying state legislators should increasingly attempt to relate the members' attitudes to their actual behavior (i.e., votes). Moreover, researchers must find more precise and definitive methods of comparing the various states' relative capacity to allocate resources to education.

A Perspective on the Future

Even the best of predictive equations may go for naught. Even if we can predict 90 percent of the variance in an educational outcome, we may still be unable to explain *or anticipate* sudden negative or positive fluctuations. As Norton Long pointed out in respect to another phenomenon, namely, the epidemic of racial disorders in the mid-sixties:

> the studies provoked by Floyd Hunter generated little expectation of the . . . upheaval. Edward Banfield's *Political Influence* indeed indicated that a serious race problem was a source of concern, but not of effective action, to some of Chicago's business leadership. Mayor Richard Lee's discomfiture [was] understandable. Sayre and

Kaufman's New York had scarcely a cloud in its sky. Most of us were clearly unprepared for what occurred. Our community-power theories and our data failed to generate appropriate expectation.[11]

Current studies of state policy making may likewise fail to provide a warning of—or even a *post hoc* explanation of—drastic change. Our perspective, therefore, on the future of education can rest only on the data obtainable at this point in time, a familiarity with relevant studies outside the scope of our own study, a knowledge of individual state trends, and lastly our hopes and expectations.

Prior studies of educational allocations gave little warning of the "taxpayers' revolt" that has in recent years dominated domestic politics. The drastic cuts in higher education budgets, the enrollment limitations, and the general education austerity that have resulted are only occasionally treated in the current literature. What observations relevant to these matters can we make on the basis of our study?

Variables relating to federal support often enter into our allocation equations for education. We would suggest that insofar as federal resources continue to be diverted into military activities, higher education will continue to suffer economic deprivations. Earlier, federal grants—whether direct, matching, or indirect—encouraged states to support higher education. Currently, state legislators, many of them influenced by the increasing radicalism on various state campuses, are attempting to remedy fiscal difficulties by limiting enrollments and by deferring important decisions to the governor, while adamantly refusing to raise new taxes to support the state system's spiraling costs.

Even among the legislators who favor tax increases for education, many prefer an increase in the sales tax, an obviously regressive tax. Informed citizens view such increases as an unwarranted addition to the tax burden of those least able to pay, and they respond by rejecting one referendum after another on school support. Usually these referendums relate to local support of schools. And, when the localities are unable to raise money to support their schools, they place an additional burden on the state legislature, thus completing the circle. Legislators and public officials may appear surprised and

[11] Norton Long, "Indicators of Change in Political Institutions," *Annals* 388 (March 1970): 38.

dismayed, but in truth they themselves have helped to create the crisis. As the opinion leaders and pace-setters for their communities, legislators should constantly strive to set good examples. When a citizen observes cynicism and self-interest dominating the highest policy councils in his state, he is unlikely to bring a charitable attitude to bear on local political decisions. A disinterest in educational needs at the state level is thus likely to engender a comparable disinterest at the local level.

The impact of the mass media, another source of public opinion, also deserves to be scrutinized more closely by scholars. Are budgets rejected because of the news media's mania for dramatizing conflicts and spotlighting controversies? Can citizens and politicians be taught to look behind the headlines for substantiation and a sense of context? Future studies on legislators, voter attitudes, and behavior should explore more fully the whole area of media impact.

Media is but a part of the technological revolution. What impact will the new educational technology have on education and attitudes toward education? If consolidation in rural school systems fails to provide the increased attention to student needs and the economies of scale promised by educators, then parents (who are also voters) will quickly become skeptical of an innovation that costs them additional money while further reducing teacher-student contact. Although income levels have thus far been positively associated with educational innovations, time may show that we have reached—or that poorer districts will soon reach—a plateau beyond which new innovations will be difficult, if not impossible, to implement. In other words, the attitude that professional educators have "experimented with our children long enough" might soon begin to gain sway over ever-increasing numbers of people. Encouraged by conservative politicians and fueled by parental frustration, this attitude might ultimately result in the wholesale rejection of the new educational technology.

In conclusion, we assert that education will in the near future become increasingly politicized. Research on the linkages between voter attitudes and voting behavior must be undertaken by a wider range of scholars and interested citizens. Educators and academicians must fulfill their obligations to the larger state society by studying the problems confronting the society, posing alternative solutions, and (if need be) leading the way out of the morass. Educational policy making is a political activity that deserves further elucidation if only because of its manifold implications for the way we govern ourselves. We trust that this study has taken us a step in that direction since certainly that was the end we had in mind.

Bibliography

Agger, Robert E.; Goldrich, Daniel; and Swanson, Bert E. *Rulers and the Ruled: Political Power and Impotence in American Communities.* New York: John Wiley, 1964.

Alford, Robert. *Party and Society.* Chicago: Rand McNally, 1963.

Anderson, Lee F.; Watts, Meridith W., Jr.; and Wilcox, Allen R. *Legislative Roll-Call Analysis.* Evanston, Ill.: Northwestern University Press, 1966.

Andreasen, Haakon L. "Teacher Unionism: Personal Data Affecting Membership." *Phi Delta Kappan* 50 (November 1968): 177.

Baer, Michael. "Environmental Effects on State Legislators and Lobbyists." Ph.D. dissertation, University of Oregon, 1968.

Bahl, Roy W., Jr., and Saunders, Robert J. "Determinants of Changes in State and Local Government Expenditures." *National Tax Journal* 18 (March 1965): 50–57.

Barton, Allen H. "Bringing Society Back In: Survey Research and Macro-Methodology." *American Behavioral Scientist* 12 (November–December 1968): 1–9.

Bauer, Raymond A., ed. *Social Indicators.* Cambridge, Mass.: The MIT Press, 1966.

————. "Social Indicators and Sample Surveys." *Public Opinion Quarterly* 30 (Fall 1966): 339–49.

Beal, George M.; Lagomarcino, Virgil; and Hartman, John J. *Iowa School*

195

Issues: Summary Report. Ames, Iowa: Department of Sociology and Anthropology, Iowa State University, 1966. Rural Sociology Report 61.

Beckett, Paul, and Sunderland, Celeste. "Washington State's Lawmakers: Some Personnel Factors in the Washington Legislature." *Western Political Quarterly* 10 (March 1957): 180–202.

Blalock, Hubert M., Jr. "Causal Inferences, Closed Populations, and Measures of Association." *American Political Science Review* 61 (March 1967): 130–36.

——————. *Social Statistics.* New York: McGraw-Hill, 1960.

Borgatta, Edgar F., ed. *Sociological Methodology 1969.* San Francisco: Jossey-Bass, 1969.

Borko, Harold, ed. *Computer Applications in the Behavioral Sciences.* Englewood Cliffs, N. J.: Prentice-Hall, 1962.

Boynton, G. R.; Patterson, Samuel C.; and Hedlund, Ronald D. "The Structure of Public Support for Legislative Institutions." *Midwest Journal of Political Science* 12 (May 1968): 163–80.

Buchanan, William. *Legislative Partisanship: The Deviant Case of California.* Berkeley, Calif.: University of California Press, 1963. University of California Publications in Political Science, Volume 13.

Campbell, Angus; Converse, Philip E.; Miller, Warren E.; and Stokes, Donald E. *The American Voter.* New York: John Wiley, 1960.

Campbell, Ernest Q., and Alexander, C. Norman. "Structural Effects and Interpersonal Relationships." *American Journal of Sociology* 71 (November 1965): 284–89.

Cattell, Raymond B., ed. *Handbook of Multivariate Experimental Psychology.* Chicago: Rand McNally, 1966.

Cawelti, Gordon, "Innovative Practices in High Schools: Who Does What—and Why—and How." *Nations Schools* 79 (April 1967): 56–88.

Chambers, M. M. "Current State Tax Support." *Phi Delta Kappan* 50 (October 1968): 113–16.

Clark, Terry N. "Community Structure, Decision-Making, Budget Expenditures, and Urban Renewal in 51 American Communities." *American Sociological Review* 33 (August 1968): 576–93.

Cnudde, Charles F., and McCrone, Donald J. "Reply to Forbes and Tufte." *American Political Science Review* 62 (December 1968): 1269–70.

Cole, Stephen. "The Unionization of Teachers: Determinants of Rank-and-File Support." *Sociology of Education* 41 (Winter 1968): 66–87.

Coleman, James S. "Relational Analysis: The Study of Social Organization with Survey Methods." *Human Organization* 17 (Winter 1958–59): 28–36.

Council of State Governments. *The Book of the States, 1964–65.* Chicago: Council of State Governments, 1966.

Crain, Robert L., and Rosenthal, Donald B. "Community Status as a Dimension of Local Decision-Making." *American Sociological Review* 32 (December 1967): 970–84.

Cushman, Robert E., and Cushman, Robert F. *Cases in Constitutional Law.* 3d ed. New York: Appleton-Century-Crofts, 1968.

Cutright, Phillips. "Political Structure, Economic Development, and National Security Programs." *American Journal of Sociology,* 70 (March 1965): 537–50.

Dahl, Robert A., and Lindblom, Charles E. *Politics, Economics and Welfare.* New York: Harper, 1953.

David, Paul T., and Eisenberg, Ralph. *Devaluation of the Urban-Suburban Vote: A Statistical Investigation of Long Term Trends in State Legislative Representation.* Charlottesville, Va.: Bureau of Public Administration, University of Virginia, 1961.

Davie, Bruce F., and Patterson, Philip D., Jr. *Vocational Education and Intergovernmental Fiscal Relations in the Post-War Period.* Washington, D.C.: Georgetown University, 1966.

Davis, Morris, and Weinbaum, Marvin G. *Metropolitan Decision Processes: An Analysis of Case Studies.* Chicago: Rand McNally, 1966.

Dawson, Richard E., and Robinson, James A. "Interparty Competition, Economic Variables, and Welfare Politics in the American States." *Journal of Politics* 25 (May 1963): 265–89.

Derge, David R. "Metropolitan and Outside Alignments in Illinois and Missouri." *American Political Science Review* 52 (December 1958): 1051–65.

Dubin, R. T. *Theory Building.* New York: The Free Press, 1969.

Duncan, Otis D. "Path Analysis: Sociological Examples." *American Journal of Sociology* 72 (July 1966): 1–16.

————; Cuzzort, Ray P.; and Duncan, Beverly. *Statistical Geography: Problems in Analyzing Areal Data.* Glencoe, Ill.: The Free Press, 1961.

Dye, Thomas R. "A Comparison of Constituency Influence in the Upper and Lower Chambers of a State Legislature." *Western Political Quarterly* 14 (June 1961): 473–80.

————. "Governmental Structure, Urban Environment, and Educational

Policy." *Midwest Journal of Political Science* 11 (February 1967): 353–80.

———. "Income Inequality and American State Politics." *American Political Science Review* 63 (March 1969): 157–62.

———. "Policy Outcomes in Public Education." Mimeographed paper presented at the Conference of Politics and Education, Center for the Advanced Study of Educational Administration, University of Oregon, 1966.

———. *Politics, Economics, and the Public: Policy Outcomes in the American States.* Chicago: Rand McNally, 1966.

Easton, David. *A Systems Analysis of Political Life.* New York: John Wiley, 1965.

Edwards, Allen. *Techniques of Attitude Construction.* New York: Appleton-Century-Crofts, 1957.

Elazar, Daniel J. *American Federalism: A View from the States.* New York: Crowell, 1966.

Eliot, Thomas H. "Toward an Understanding of Public School Politics." *American Political Science Review* 53 (December 1959): 1032–51.

Etzioni, Amitai, ed. *Complex Organizations.* New York: Holt, Rinehart & Winston, 1961.

Eulau, Heinz. "Bases of Authority in Legislative Bodies." *Administrative Science Quarterly* 7 (December 1962): 309–21.

———. "The Ecological Basis of Party Systems: The Case of Ohio." *Midwest Journal of Politics* 1 (August 1957): 125–35.

Evans, John C., Jr. *Utah School Crisis, 1963.* Salt Lake City: Utah Education Association, 1963.

Faris, Robert E. L., ed. *Handbook of Modern Sociology.* Chicago: Rand McNally, 1964.

Fenton, John H. *Midwest Politics.* New York: Holt, Rinehart & Winston, 1966.

Ferguson, LeRoy Craig. *How State Legislators View the Problem of School Needs.* East Lansing, Mich.: Cooperative Research Projects, Michigan State University, 1960. Project No. 532.

Fishbein, Martin, ed. *Readings in Attitude Theory and Measurement.* New York: John Wiley, 1967.

Fisher, Glen W. "Interstate Variation in State and Local Government Expenditures." *National Tax Journal* 17 (March 1964): 57–74.

Forbes, Hugh Donald, and Tufte, Edward R. "A Note of Caution on Causal Modeling." *American Political Science Review* 62 (December 1968): 1258–64.

Francis, Wayne L. *Legislative Issues in the Fifty States.* Chicago: Rand McNally, 1967.

Freeman, Linton C. *Elementary Applied Statistics: For Students in Behavioral Science.* New York: John Wiley, 1965.

Garnsey, Morris E. *America's New Frontier: The Mountain West.* New York: Alfred A. Knopf, 1950.

Goldberger, Arthur S. "On Boudon's Method of Linear Causal Analysis." *American Sociological Review* 35 (February 1970): 97–101.

Golembiewski, Robert T.; Welsh, William A.; and Crotty, William J. *A Methodological Primer for Political Scientists.* Chicago: Rand McNally, 1969.

Gordon, Robert A. "Issues in Multiple Regression." *American Journal of Sociology* 73 (March 1968): 592–616.

Grieder, Calvin. "New Conant Plan Raises Some Searching Questions." *Nations Schools* 82 (November 1968): 6.

Gross, Neal; Mason, Ward S.; and McEachern, Alexander W. *Explorations in Role Analysis.* New York: John Wiley, 1958.

Grumm, John. "A Factor Analysis of Legislative Behavior." *Midwest Journal of Political Science* 7 (November 1963): 336–56.

————. "Structural Determinants of Legislative Output." Mimeographed paper presented at the Conference on the Measurement of Public Policies in the United States, University of Michigan, Ann Arbor, Michigan, 28 July–3 August 1968.

Hagedon, Robert, and Labovitz, Sanford. "Participation in Community Associations by Occupation: A Test of Three Theories." *American Sociological Review* 33 (April 1968): 272–83.

Hays, William L. *Statistics for Psychologists.* New York: Holt, Rinehart & Winston, 1963.

Heard, Alexander, ed. *State Legislatures in American Politics.* Englewood Cliffs, N. J.: Prentice-Hall, 1966.

Hofferbert, Richard I. "Ecological Development and Policy Change in the American States." *Midwest Journal of Political Science* 10 (November 1966): 464–83.

————. "Socioeconomic Dimensions of American States: 1890-1960." *Midwest Journal of Political Science* 12 (August 1968): 401–18.

————. "The Relation Between Public Policy and Some Structural and Environmental Variables in the American States." *American Political Science Review* 60 (March 1966): 73–82.

Hyneman, Charles S. "Who Makes Our Laws?" *Political Science Quarterly* 55 (December 1940): 556–81.

Jacob, Herbert, and Vines, Kenneth N., eds. *Politics in the American States: A Comparative Analysis.* Boston: Little, Brown, 1965.

James, H. Thomas; Kelly, James A.; and Garms, Walter I. *Determinants of Educational Expenditures in Large Cities in the United States.* East Lansing, Mich.: Cooperative Research Projects, Michigan State University, 1966. Project No. 2389.

————; Thomas, J. Alan; and Dyck, Harold J. *Wealth, Expenditures and Decision-Making for Education.* Stanford, Calif.: Cooperative Research Projects, School of Education, Stanford University, 1963. Project No. 1241.

Jewell, Malcolm E. *The State Legislature.* New York: Random House, 1962.

————. *Legislative Representation in the Contemporary South.* Durham, N. C.: Duke University Press, 1967.

————, and Patterson, Samuel C. *The Legislative Process in the United States.* New York: Random House, 1966.

Jonas, Frank H., ed. *Western Politics.* Salt Lake City: University of Utah Press, 1961.

Keefe, William J. "Parties, Partisanship, and Public Policy in the Pennsylvania Legislature." *American Political Science Review* 48 (June 1954): 450–64.

Key, V. O. *Public Opinion and American Democracy.* New York: Alfred A. Knopf, 1961.

————. *Southern Politics in State and Nation.* New York: Vintage Books, 1949.

Labovitz, Sanford. "Some Observations on Measurement and Statistics." *Social Forces* 46 (December 1967): 151–60.

Lipset, Seymour M. *Political Man.* New York: Doubleday, 1960.

Lockard, Duane. *New England Politics.* Princeton, N.J.: Princeton University Press, 1959.

Long, Norton. "Indicators of Change in Political Institutions." *Annals,* 388 (March 1970): 35–45.

Luttbeg, Norman, ed. *Public Opinion and Public Policy.* Homewood, Ill.: The Dorsey Press, 1968.

————, and Zeigler, Harmon. "Attitude Consensus and Conflict in an Interest Group." *American Political Science Review* 60 (September 1966): 655–66.

McClosky, Herbert. "Consensus and Ideology in American Politics." *American Political Science Review* 58 (June 1964): 361–82.

————; Hoffman, Paul J.; and O'Hara, Rosemary. "Issue Conflict and Consensus Among Party Leaders and Followers." *American Political Science Review* 54 (June 1960): 406–27.

Marvick, Dwaine, ed. *Political Decision-Makers.* Glencoe, Ill.: The Free Press, 1961.

Masotti, Louis H. "Intergovernmental Relations and the Socialization of Conflict: Interest Articulation in the Politics of Education." Mimeographed paper presented at the 1967 Midwest Conference of Political Scientists, Purdue, Indiana, 27–29 April 1967.

Masters, Nicholas A.; Salisbury, Robert H.; and Eliot, Thomas H. *State Politics and the Public Schools: An Exploratory Analysis.* New York: Alfred A. Knopf, 1964.

Maxwell, James A. *Financing State and Local Government.* Washington, D.C.: Brookings Institute, 1965.

Meranto, Philip. *The Politics of Federal Aid to Education in 1965: A Study in Political Innovation.* Syracuse, N.Y.: Syracuse University Press, 1967.

Miller, James Nathan. "Hamstrung Legislatures." *National Civic Review* 54 (April 1965): 180–82.

Miner, Jerry. *Social and Economic Factors in Spending for Public Education.* Syracuse, N.Y.: Syracuse University Press, 1963.

Morss, Elliot R. "Some Thoughts on the Determinants of State and Local Expenditures." *National Tax Journal* 19 (March 1966): 95–103.

Muir, J. Douglas. "The Tough New Teacher." *American School Board Journal* 156 (November 1968): 9–14.

National Education Association. *Utah: A State-Wide Study of School Conditions.* National Commission on Professional Rights and Responsibilities, 1964.

Newcomb, Theodore M.; Turner, Ralph H.; and Converse, Philip E. *Social Psychology: A Study of Human Interaction.* New York: Holt, Rinehart & Winston, 1960.

Orbell, John M., with Sherrill, Kenneth S. "Racial Attitudes and the Metropolitan Context." *Public Opinion Quarterly* 33 (Spring 1969): 46–54.

Patterson, Samuel C. "Legislative Leadership and Political Ideology." *Public Opinion Quarterly* 27 (Fall 1963): 399–410.

————. "Patterns of Interpersonal Relations in a State Legislative Group: The Wisconsin Assembly." *Public Opinion Quarterly* 23 (Spring 1959): 101–9.

Perloff, Harvey S., *et. al. Regions, Resources, and Economic Growth.* Baltimore: Johns Hopkins University Press, 1962.

Ranney, David C. "The Impact of Metropolitanism on Central City Education." *Educational Administration Quarterly* 5 (Winter 1969): 24–36.

Rummel, R. J. "Understanding Factor Analysis." *Journal of Conflict Resolution* 11 (December 1967): 448–51.

Russett, Bruce M. "Social Change and Attitudes on Development and the Political System in India." *Journal of Politics* 29 (August 1967): 483–504.

Sacks, Seymour, and Harris, Robert. "The Determinants of State and Local Government Expenditures and Intergovernmental Flow of Funds." *National Tax Journal* 17 (March 1964): 75–85.

Shannon, Lyle W. "Is Level of Development Related to Capacity for Self-Government?" *American Journal of Economics and Sociology* 17 (1958): 367–82.

Sharkansky, Ira. "Economic and Political Correlates of State Government Expenditures: General Tendencies and Deviant Cases." *Midwest Journal of Political Science* 11 (May 1967): 173–79.

_____. "Regional Patterns in the Expenditures of American States." *Western Political Quarterly* 20 (December 1967): 955–71.

_____. "Some More Thoughts About the Determinants of Government Expenditures." *National Tax Journal* 20 (June 1967): 171–79.

_____. *Spending in the United States.* Chicago: Rand McNally, 1968.

Sigel, Roberta S., and Friesema, H. Paul. "Urban Community Leaders' Knowledge of Public Opinion." *Western Political Quarterly* 18 (December 1965): 881–95.

Smith, Arthur K., Jr. "Socio-Economic Development and Political Democracy: A Causal Analysis." *Midwest Journal of Political Science* 13 (February 1969): 95–125.

Somers, Robert H. "A New Asymmetric Measure of Association for Ordinal Variables." *American Sociological Review* 27 (December 1962): 799–811.

Sorauf, Frank J. *Party and Representation: Legislative Politics in Pennsylvania.* New York: Atherton Press, 1963.

Stinnett, T. M. *Turmoil in Teaching.* New York: Macmillan, 1968.

U. S. Bureau of the Census. *Statistical Abstract of the United States: 1968.* Washington, D.C.: Government Printing Office, 1968.

Usdan, Michael D. "The Role and Future of State Educational Coalitions." *Educational Administration Quarterly* 5 (Spring 1969): 26–42.

Wahlke, John C.; Buchanan, William; Eulau, Heinz; and Ferguson, LeRoy Craig. "American State Legislators' Role Orientations Toward Pressure Groups." *Journal of Politics* 22 (May 1960), 203–27.

————; Eulau, Heinz; Buchanan, William; and Ferguson, LeRoy Craig. *The Legislative System: Explorations in Legislative Behavior.* New York: John Wiley, 1962.

Zeigler, Harmon, and Baer, Michael. *Lobbying: Interaction and Influence in American State Legislatures.* Belmont, Calif.: Wadsworth, 1969.

————, and Johnson, Karl F. "Educational Innovations and Politico-Economic Systems." *Education and Urban Society* 1 (February 1969): 161–76.

Zelditch, Morris. *A Basic Course in Sociological Statistics.* New York: Holt, Rinehart & Winston, 1966.

Zetterberg, Hans L. *On Theory and Verification in Sociology.* 3d ed. New York: Bedminster Press, 1964.

appendix A

List of Variables and Data Sources

(Note: Not all of the variables listed here appear in the regression equations in Chapter 3. These were the variables that constituted the final factor analysis, from which the progressive liberalism and federalism-and-concern factors emerged.)

	Variable	*Source*
1.	Biennial compensation of legislators based on typical length of session, 1964–65	3
2.	Length of regular session in calendar days, 1963–64	3
3.	Length of regular session plus extra sessions, in calendar days, 1963–64	3
4.	Average population per senate district, 1960	Computed
5.	Number of bills introduced in 1961–62, regular and extra sessions	3
6.	Number of bills enacted into law in 1963–64, regular and extra sessions	3

Variable	*Source*
7. Expenditures on the legislative branch, 1963–64 biennium	3
8. Per capita expenditures on the legislative branch, 1963–64 biennium	3
9. Expenditures on compensation of legislators, 1963–64 biennium	3
10. Per capita expenditures on compensation of legislators, 1963–64 biennium	3
11. Expenditures on legislative services and operations, 1963–64 biennium	3
12. Party competition index for senate, 1963–64 (minority party percentage of two-party membership multiplied by two)	3
13. Party competition index for lower house, 1963–64 (computed as in 12)	3
14. Democratic percentage of two-party membership in lower house, 1961–62	3
15. Democratic percentage of two-party membership in senate, 1963–64	3
16. Democratic percentage of two-party membership in lower house, 1963–64	3
17. Ranney index of interparty competition, 1946–53	15
18. Percentage of population increase, 1960–63	23
19. Net migration from 1960 to 1963 divided by 1960 population related to a base of 100 (100 = no migration)	23
20. Negro percentage of population, 1960	23
21. Median age of population, 1960	23
22. Median school years completed by persons over twenty-five, 1960	23

Variable	*Source*
23. College enrollment per 10,000 population, 1964	23
24. Foreign and mixed parentage as a percentage of total population, 1960	23
25. Urban population, percentage of population residing in state's largest single Standard Metropolitan Statistical Area (SMSA), 1963	6
26. Sound housing, percentage of total, 1960	23
27. Draft board mental test, percentage of failures, 1963	12
28. Population per lawyer, 1963	23
29. Number of telephones per 1,000 population, 1963	23
30. Workers who walk to work as a percentage of total population, 1960	17
31. Estimated market value of property per capita, 1961	23
32. Per capita income, 1963	23
33. Per capita value added by manufacturing, 1963	23
34. Construction expenditures per capita, 1963	23
35. Average acreage per farm, 1959	23
36. Retail sales per capita, 1963	12
37. Total federal expenditures per capita, fiscal 1963	17
38. Federal defense expenditures per capita, fiscal 1963	23
39. Federal grants to state and local governments per capita, fiscal 1963	23
40. Federal income and employment tax collections per capita, fiscal 1963	23

Variable	*Source*
41. State and local taxes per capita, fiscal 1963	23
42. State and local taxes per $1,000 of personal income, fiscal 1963	23
43. Percentage of state and local revenues from federal government, fiscal 1963	23
44. State general revenues per capita, fiscal 1964	28
45. State taxes per capita, fiscal 1964	28
46. State debt outstanding per capita, fiscal 1964	28
47. Measure of inequality of racial opportunity	32
48. Public school expenditures per pupil, fiscal 1963	23
49. Public school expenditures per $1,000 of personal income, fiscal 1964	28
50. Number of students per classroom, 1964	23
51. Old age assistance, average monthly payment per recipient, December 1964	23
52. Aid to dependent children, average monthly payment per recipient, December 1964	23
53. Aid to the blind, average monthly payment per recipient, December 1964	23
54. Unemployment compensation, average weekly payment per recipient, fiscal 1963	3
55. Per capita expenditures for higher education, fiscal 1963	23
56. Expenditures per 1,000 recipients of public welfare, fiscal 1964	18
57. Voter turnout in gubernatorial and senatorial elections in non-Presidential election years, 1952–60	10
58. Democratic percentage of two-party vote for President, 1964	23

	Variable	*Source*
59.	Change in per capita state and local expenditures for health services and hospitals, fiscal 1953–63 (1953 = 100)	18
60.	Change in length of regular sessions, 1951–52 to 1961–62 (1951–52 = 100)	3
61.	Change in college enrollment, 1950–60 (1950 = 100)	23
62.	Change in state and local per capita tax collections, fiscal 1953–63 (percentage of increase)	23
63.	Change in per capita income, 1950–60 (percentage of increase)	23
64.	Change in value added by agriculture, 1950–60 (1950 = 100)	23
65.	Change in value added by manufacturing, 1954–63 (percentage of increase)	23
66.	Change in expenditures for new plant and equipment, 1954–63 (percentage of increase)	23
67.	Change in percentage of Negro population, 1950–63 (100 plus percentage of increase or decrease)	23
68.	Median family income, 1959	19
69.	Percentage of membership in senate from majority party, 1954–62	27
70.	Average winning percentage in gubernatorial elections, 1954–62	27
71.	Votes cast for U.S. Representative as percentage of voting age population, 1962	22
72.	Federal percentage of total educational expenditures, fiscal 1961	30
73.	Per capita educational expenditures of state and local governments, fiscal 1961	22

Variable	*Source*
74. General assistance, average monthly payment per case, December 1961	21
75. Old age assistance, recipients per 100,000 population, December 1961	21
76. Patients in public mental hospitals per 100,000 population, 1960	22
77. Per capita expenditures of state and local governments for public welfare, fiscal 1961	22
78. Percentage of state and local funds allocated to public welfare, fiscal 1961	22
79. Per capita state expenditures for welfare, fiscal 1961	22
80. Per capita community chest donations, 1961	21
81. Per capita federal grants to state and local governments for health, welfare, and related activities, fiscal 1961	21
82. State and local revenues per capita, fiscal 1961	22
83. State and local tax revenues per capita, fiscal 1961	22
84. Local tax revenues per capita, fiscal 1961	22
85. Per capita state expenditures for correctional system, fiscal 1961	22
86. State and local expenditures for welfare as a percentage of personal income, 1961	22
87. Pari-mutuel and gambling receipts as a percentage of total state revenues, fiscal 1962	17
88. Per capita state and local expenditures for highways, fiscal 1961	22
89. Percentage of state and local funds allocated to highways, fiscal 1961	22
90. State and local expenditures for highways as a percentage of personal income, 1961	22

Variable	*Source*
91. Per capita state expenditures for highways, fiscal 1961	22
92. State percentage of total highway expenditures, fiscal 1961	22
93. Percentage of state highway funds from federal government, fiscal 1961	22
94. Per capita highway funds from federal government, fiscal 1961	22
95. Democratic percentage of membership in lower house, 1963	22
96. Democratic percentage of membership in senate, 1963	22
97. Average Democratic percentage in gubernatorial elections, 1956–62	22
98. Federal percentage of total welfare expenditures, fiscal 1961	22
99. General assistance cases as a percentage of total population, 1961	22
100. Number of bills introduced in Congress, 1961–62	22
101. Number of bills enacted by Congress, 1961–62	22
102. Total highway mileage, 1961	22
103. Interstate highway system designated mileage, 1961	22
104. Federal primary system mileage, 1961	20
105. Number of governments per person, 1961	22
106. Federal percentage of total highway funds, 1961	29
107. Aid to the blind, recipients per 100,000 population, December 1961	21

Variable	*Source*
108. Aid to the disabled, recipients per 100,000 population, December 1961	21
109. Municipalities and special districts per 10,000 population, 1962	22
110. Paroled prisoners as a percentage of all releases, 1960	2
111. Gini index, 1959	5
112. Hofferbert factor score, Table III: Industrialization, 1960	8
113. Hofferbert factor score, Table IV: Cultural enrichment, 1960	8
114. National Education Association membership, percentage of public school personnel in state, June 1966	16
115. American Federation of Teachers membership, percentage of public school personnel in state, June 1966	16
116. State's share of federal funds under Section 4 of the Vocational Education Act of 1963, fiscal 1965	4
117. Funds spent as a percentage of Section 4 funds available under the 1963 Vocational Act, by state, fiscal 1965	4
118. Percentage of Vocational Act funds allocated to secondary schools, fiscal 1965*	4
119. Percentage of Vocational Act funds allocated to postsecondary education, fiscal 1965*	4
120. Percentage of Vocational Act funds allocated to adult education, fiscal 1965*	4
121. Percentage of Vocational Act funds allocated to construction, fiscal 1965*	4

* On the Vocational Act distributions, figures less than 0.5 were given a .001 reading to ensure that there would be no zero categories.

Variable	Source
122. Number of state-required courses, 1966	9
123. General innovations score	31
124. Educational innovations score, 1966	1
125. Public school expenditures per pupil, fiscal 1964	23
126. Public school expenditures per pupil, fiscal 1965	24
127. Per capita educational expenditures of state and local governments, fiscal 1965	24
128. Per capita educational expenditures of state and local governments, fiscal 1966	26
129. Number of pupils enrolled in elementary schools, 1965	24
130. Number of pupils enrolled in secondary schools, 1965	23
131. Number of classrooms available and in use, 1965	23
132. Number of pupils enrolled in elementary schools, 1966	25
133. Number of pupils enrolled in secondary schools, 1966	25
134. Number of classrooms available and in use, 1966	25
135. Percentage of school revenues derived from state, fiscal 1964	13
136. Percentage of school revenues derived from state, fiscal 1965	14
137. Expenditures for higher education (current operations), fiscal 1964	26
138. Population, 1963	26

Variable	Source
139. Expenditures for higher education (current operations), fiscal 1966	7
140. Population, 1965	26
141. Expenditures for higher education (plant expansion), fiscal 1964	26
142. Population, 1961	26
143. Per capita expenditures for higher education, fiscal 1964 (137 divided by 138)	Computed
144. Per capita expenditures for higher education, fiscal 1966 (139 divided by 140)	Computed
145. Number of students per classroom, 1965 (the sum of 129 and 130 divided by 131)	Computed
146. Number of students per classroom, 1966 (the sum of 132 and 133 divided by 134)	Computed

Data Sources

1. Cawelti, Gordon. "Innovative Practices in High Schools: Who Does What—and Why—and How." *Nations Schools* 79 (April 1967): 56–88.

2. Council of State Governments. *The Book of the States: 1962–63*. Chicago: Council of State Governments, 1962.

3. _____. *The Book of the States: 1964–65*. Chicago: Council of State Governments, 1964.

4. Davie, Bruce F., and Patterson, Philip D., Jr. *Vocational Education and Intergovernmental Fiscal Relations in the Post-War Period*. Washington, D.C.: Georgetown University, 1966.

5. Dye, Thomas R. "Income Inequality and American State Politics." *American Political Science Review* 63 (March 1969): 157–62.

6. Executive Office of the President, Bureau of the Budget, *Standard Metropolitan Statistical Areas*. Washington, D.C.: Government Printing Office, 1964.

Data Sources

7. Harrington, Wells (head of the Statistical Reference Group, National Center for Educational Statistics). Personal Communication. Washington, D.C.: Office of Education, Department of Health, Education, and Welfare, January 1968.

8. Hofferbert, Richard I. "Socioeconomic Dimensions of American States: 1890–1960." *Midwest Journal of Political Science* 12 (August 1968): 401–18.

9. Marconnet, George D. "State Legislatures and the School Curriculum." *Phi Delta Kappan* 49 (January 1968): 269–72.

10. Milbrath, Lester. "Political Participation in the States." In *Politics in the American States,* edited by Herbert Jacob and Kenneth N. Vines. Boston: Little, Brown, 1965.

11. National Education Association. *National Education Association Handbook, 1966–67.* Washington, D.C.: National Education Association, 1967.

12. _____. *Rankings of the States: 1965.* Washington, D.C.: National Education Association, 1965.

13. _____, Research Division. *NEA Research Bulletin* 42 (December 1964). Washington, D.C.: National Education Association, 1964.

14. _____. *NEA Research Bulletin* 44 (February 1966). Washington, D.C.: National Education Association, 1966.

15. Ranney, Austin. "Parties in State Politics." In *Politics in the American States,* edited by Herbert Jacob and Kenneth N. Vines. Boston: Little, Brown, 1965.

16. Stinnett, T. M. *Turmoil in Teaching: A History of the Organizational Struggle for America's Teachers.* New York: Macmillan, 1968.

17. U.S. Bureau of the Census. *Compendium of State Government Finances in 1962.* Washington, D.C.: Government Printing Office, 1963.

18. _____. *Compendium of State Government Finances in 1964.* Washington, D.C.: Government Printing Office, 1965.

Data Sources

19. _____. *Statistical Abstract of the United States: 1960*. 81st ed. Washington, D.C.: Government Printing Office, 1960.

20. _____. *Statistical Abstract of the United States: 1961*. 82d ed. Washington, D.C.: Government Printing Office, 1961.

21. _____. *Statistical Abstract of the United States: 1962*. 83d ed. Washington, D.C.: Government Printing Office, 1962.

22. _____. *Statistical Abstract of the United States: 1963*. 84th ed. Washington, D.C.: Government Printing Office, 1963.

23. _____. *Statistical Abstract of the United States: 1965*. 86th ed. Washington, D.C.: Government Printing Office, 1965.

24. _____. *Statistical Abstract of the United States: 1966*. 87th ed. Washington, D.C.: Government Printing Office, 1966.

25. _____. *Statistical Abstract of the United States: 1967*. 88th ed. Washington, D.C.: Government Printing Office, 1967.

26. _____. *Statistical Abstract of the United States: 1968*. 89th ed. Washington, D.C.: Government Printing Office, 1968.

27. _____. *Statistical Abstract of the United States 1956–63*. Computed summaries. Washington, D.C.: Government Printing Office, 1956–63.

28. U.S. Congress, Senate, Committee on Governmental Operations. *Federal Expenditures to States and Regions*. 89th Cong., 2d sess., 1966.

29. U.S. Bureau of Public Roads. *Highway Statistics, 1962*. Washington, D.C.: Government Printing Office, 1962.

30. Hobson, Carol Joy, and Schloss, Samuel. *Statistics of State School Systems, 1961–62*. Washington, D.C.: U.S. Department of Health, Education, and Welfare, Office of Education, 1964.

31. Walker, Jack L. "The Diffusion of Innovations Among the American States." *American Political Science Review* 58 (September 1969): 880–99.

32. Wilson, John Oliver. "Inequality of Racial Opportunity—An Excursion into the New Frontier of Socioeconomic Indicators." Mimeographed.

appendix B

National Mean, Standard Deviation, and Areal Tables for Selected Variables

Variable	Mean	Standard Deviation
Per capita expenditures on the legislative branch, 1963–64 biennium: x_8	1.13	1.01
Per capita expenditures on compensation of legislators, 1963–64 biennium: x_{10}	.42	.45
Party competition index for senate, 1963–64: x_{12}	59.44	24.55
Party competition index for lower house, 1963–64: x_{13}	61.51	27.91
Democratic percentage of two-party membership in senate, 1963–64: x_{15}	74.22	10.32
Democratic percentage of two-party membership in lower house, 1963–64: x_{16}	63.67	30.44
Negro percentage of population, 1960: x_{20}	8.83	10.44
Median age of population, 1960: x_{21}	28.37	2.68

Variable	Mean	Standard Deviation
Median school years completed by persons over twenty-five, 1960: x_{22}	10.59	1.09
College enrollment per 10,000 population, 1964: x_{23}	2507.4	655.9
Foreign and mixed parentage as a percentage of total population, 1960: x_{24}	12.47	8.39
Urban population, percentage of population residing in state's largest SMSA, 1963: x_{25}	28.31	18.35
Draft board mental test, percentage of failures, 1963: x_{27}	22.14	13.19
Population per lawyer, 1963: x_{28}	814.00	200.78
Number of telephones per 1,000 population, 1963: x_{29}	407.10	78.93
Estimated market value of property per capita, 1961: x_{31}	4913.60	1270.74
Per capita income, 1963: x_{32}	2301.94	463.26
Retail sales per capita, 1963: x_{36}	1254.8	179.7
Federal grants to state and local governments per capita, 1963: x_{39}	56.10	26.60
Federal income and employment tax collections per capita, 1963: x_{40}	299.80	143.08
State and local taxes per capita, 1963: x_{41}	220.94	44.75
Percentage of state and local revenues from federal government: x_{43}	17.23	5.83
State general revenues per capita, 1964: x_{44}	229.40	89.40
Public school expenditures per pupil, 1963: x_{48}	411.24	95.27

Variable	Mean	Standard Deviation
Number of students per classroom, 1964: x_{50}	26.01	2.47
Old age assistance, average monthly payment per recipient, December 1964: x_{51}	78.72	15.71
Aid to the blind, average monthly payment per recipient, December 1964: x_{53}	86.76	20.95
Expenditures for higher education per capita, 1963: x_{55}	30.50	15.37
Voter turnout in gubernatorial and senatorial elections in non-Presidential years, 1952–60: x_{57}	44.32	17.54
Democratic percentage of two-party vote for President, 1964: x_{58}	56.16	13.09
Change in per capita income, 1950–60: x_{63}	49.26	9.37
Change in value added by agriculture, 1950–60: x_{64}	135.65	21.73
Change in percentage of Negro population, 1950–63: x_{67}	100.11	1.41
Median family income, 1959: x_{68}	5352.50	1009.32
Percentage of membership in senate from majority party, 1954–62: x_{69}	73.50	16.62
Average winning percentage in gubernatorial elections, 1954–62: x_{70}	60.61	13.32
Federal percentage of total educational expenditures, 1961: x_{72}	6.21	3.92
Per capita educational expenditures of state and local governments, 1961: x_{73}	114.06	26.86

Variable	Mean	Standard Deviation
General assistance, average monthly payment per case, December 1961: x_{74}	52.34	23.96
State and local revenues per capita, 1961: x_{82}	296.48	61.63
State and local tax revenues per capita, 1961: x_{83}	200.32	42.25
Per capita state expenditures for correctional system, 1961: x_{85}	2.80	1.21
State and local expenditures for welfare as a percentage of personal income, 1961: x_{86}	14.40	14.58
Democratic percentage of membership in lower house, 1963: x_{95}	62.08	23.66
Democratic percentage of membership in senate, 1963: x_{96}	61.13	25.89
Average Democratic percentage in gubernatorial elections, 1956–62: x_{97}	61.51	27.91
Federal percentage of total welfare expenditures: x_{98}	56.34	13.31
General assistance cases as a percentage of total population: x_{99}	.19	.13
Aid to the disabled recipients per 100,000 population, December 1961: x_{108}	25.65	15.92
Paroled prisoners as a percentage of all releases, 1960: x_{110}	55.10	25.28
Gini index, 1959: x_{111}	.39	.27
Cultural enrichment, Hofferbert factor, 1960: x_{113}	45.10	9.35
National Education Association membership, percentage of public school personnel in state, June 1966: x_{114}	54.94	10.91

Variable	Mean	Standard Deviation
American Federation of Teachers membership, percentage of public school personnel in state, June 1966: x_{115}	4.96	5.93
Percentage of Vocational Act funds allocated to postsecondary education, 1965: x_{119}	19.17	20.07
Percentage of Vocational Act funds allocated to adult education, 1965: x_{120}	7.33	12.15
General innovation: x_{123}	.45	.86
Educational innovation, 1966: x_{124}	5.99	1.34
Public school expenditures per pupil, 1964: x_{125}	459.88	108.22
Public school expenditures per pupil, 1965: x_{126}	505.40	137.02
Per capita educational expenditures of state and local governments, 1965: x_{127}	153.00	37.32
Per capita educational expenditures of state and local governments, 1966: x_{128}	155.18	38.36
Percentage of school revenues from state, 1964: x_{135}	44.17	20.42
Percentage of school revenues from state, 1965: x_{136}	44.16	24.20
Expenditures for higher education per capita, 1964: x_{143}	45.36	14.95
Expenditures for higher education per capita, 1966: x_{144}	61.05	22.95
Number of students per classroom, 1965: x_{145}	25.63	2.39
Number of students per classroom, 1966: x_{146}	25.23	4.41

Table B–1 Comparison of Areal Units on Dependent Variable:
Per Capita Educational Expenditures of State and Local Governments, 1961

State	y_{73}	$\bar{y}$	x_{82}	x_{21}	x_{23}	x_{63}	x_{24}	x_{68}	x_{28}	x_{115}	x_{98}	x_{12}	x_{120}
								Variable					
Massachusetts	90	107.76	315	321	336	510	288	6272	482	84	401	700	5.5
Connecticut	102	107.75	291	318	254	510	279	6887	607	64	340	722	19
North Carolina	87	68.88	209	255	193	560	10	3956	1230	0	711	800	2
South Carolina	78	72.26	202	234	150	580	11	3821	1286	0	735	0	331
Oregon	145	130.56	298	308	316	410	130	5892	682	13	456	600	15
Washington	148	87.17	347	296	303	390	166	6225	804	25	399	694	209
Utah	162	166.16	310	229	498	490	120	5899	865	0	550	959	27
Arizona	138	73.10	318	251	378	550	12	5568	816	22	670	286	18

221

Table B-2 Comparison of Areal Units on Educational Variable: Educational Innovation, 1966

State	y_{124}	$\bar{y}$	x_{32}	x_{25}	x_{67}	x_{58}	x_{98}	x_{97}	x_{13}	x_{29}
						Variable				
Massachusetts	7.7	7.99	2853	497	100.6	765	12.0	50.8	75.0	502
Connecticut	8.6	7.33	3185	206	101.5	679	7.1	55.0	75.5	544
North Carolina	5.3	2.96	1807	67	98.7	562	8.4	60.7	35.0	296
South Carolina	5.6	3.88	1588	105	96.0	411	6.8	99.9	0	274
Oregon	6.8	6.35	2502	399	100.3	639	7.5	46.0	96.7	448
Washington	6.6	6.61	2484	362	100.4	624	10.3	53.0	97.0	445
Utah	7.2	5.54	2119	456	100.1	547	6.6	54.6	96.8	429
Arizona	3.3	3.17	2142	426	100.2	495	5.9	48.7	80.0	354

Table B-3 Comparison of Areal Units on Dependent Variable:
American Federation of Teachers Membership, June 1966

State	y_{115}	$\bar{y}$	x_{25}	x_{24}	x_{40}	x_{12}	x_{99}	x_{13}	x_{83}	x_{108}	x_{63}	x_{51}	x_{97}
Massachusetts	8.4	17.81	497	28.8	406	700	13.6	75.0	251	14	51	96	50.8
Connecticut	6.4	9.55	206	27.9	459	722	16.5	75.5	223	9	51	81	55.0
North Carolina	0	10.07	67	1.0	187	800	3.9	35.0	144	45	56	61	60.7
South Carolina	0	10.18	105	1.1	135	0	6.5	0	132	34	58	52	99.9
Oregon	1.3	10.21	399	13.0	293	600	26.3	96.7	221	27	41	71	46.0
Washington	2.5	13.85	362	16.6	352	694	45.6	97.0	240	25	39	83	53.0
Utah	0	16.15	456	12.0	306	959	17.2	96.8	208	36	49	69	54.6
Arizona	2.2	4.70	426	1.5	157	286	27.4	80.0	212	0	55	63	48.7

223

Table B-4 Comparison of Areal Units on Dependent Variable:
National Education Association Membership, June 1966

State	y_{114}	$\bar{y}$	x_{24}	x_{13}	x_{40}	x_{99}	x_{12}
				Variable			
Massachusetts	29	49.78	28.8	75.0	406	13.6	700
Connecticut	29	48.54	27.9	75.5	459	16.5	722
North Carolina	76	47.57	1.0	35.0	182	3.9	800
South Carolina	52	66.03	1.1	0	135	6.5	0
Oregon	91	70.18	13.0	96.7	293	26.3	600
Washington	101	32.09	16.6	97.0	352	45.6	694
Utah	84	67.99	12.0	96.8	306	17.2	959
Arizona	81	80.28	1.2	80.0	219	27.4	286

Table B–5 Comparison of Areal Units on Dependent Variable:
Percentage of Vocational Act Funds Allocated to Adult Education, 1965

State	y_{120}	$\bar{y}$	*Variable* x_{70}	x_{74}	x_{111}
Massachusetts	5.5	6.18	52.2	72	414
Connecticut	1.9	7.12	55.0	68	404
North Carolina	.2	12.68	63.0	190	465
South Carolina	33.1	30.19	99.9	29	474
Oregon	1.5	2.57	54.2	50	411
Washington	20.9	9.30	52.8	84	413
Utah	2.7	6.78	55.3	66	394
Arizona	1.8	4.33	56.9	48	445

Table B–6 Comparison of Areal Units on Dependent Variable:
Percentage of Vocational Act Funds Allocated to Postsecondary Education, 1965

State	Variable			
	y_{119}	$\bar{y}$	x_{86}	x_{64}
Massachusetts	2.4	9.96	15	93
Connecticut	33.4	6.71	8	99
North Carolina	2.3	11.74	10	143
South Carolina	0	16.73	9	142
Oregon	24.1	17.81	12	138
Washington	33.4	24.39	16	156
Utah	20.9	13.24	11	120
Arizona	47.8	27.84	10	190

Table B–7 Comparison of Areal Units on Dependent Variable:
Public School Expenditures Per Pupil, 1963

State	y_{48}	$\bar{y}$	x_{68}	x_{41}	x_{63}	x_{31}	x_{21}	x_{57}	x_{73}	x_{99}
						Variable				
Massachusetts	465	501.87	6272	270	510	4860	321	58.8	90	13.6
Connecticut	533	541.46	6887	264	510	3540	318	63.4	102	16.5
North Carolina	296	264.80	3956	166	560	4870	255	25.1	87	3.9
South Carolina	260	251.63	3821	141	580	2480	234	11.9	78	6.5
Oregon	518	500.35	5892	243	410	5670	308	55.9	145	26.3
Washington	495	502.29	6225	271	390	6390	296	52.6	148	45.6
Utah	351	392.22	5899	222	490	4430	229	64.3	162	17.2
Arizona	430	383.46	5568	246	550	5740	251	43.5	138	27.4

Table B-8 Comparison of Areal Units on Dependent Variable:
Public School Expenditures Per Pupil, 1964

State	y_{125}	$\bar{y}$	X_{48}	X_{41}	X_{53}	X_{25}	X_{110}	X_{115}	X_{27}	X_{95}	X_{22}	X_{28}	X_{29}	X_{51}	X_{113}
Mass.	528	495.80	465	270	136	497	64.9	84	14.1	58.9	11.6	482	502	96	321
Conn.	600	674.62	533	264	102	206	86.2	64	16.4	34.5	11.0	607	544	81	690
N.C.	322	316.87	296	166	66	67	32.8	0	43.8	88.7	8.9	1230	296	61	−1627
S.C.	284	278.34	260	141	63	105	17.9	0	50.7	99.9	8.7	1286	274	52	−2050
Oreg.	569	565.38	518	243	90	399	42.5	13	6.9	52.0	11.8	682	448	71	966
Wash.	534	525.28	495	271	102	362	94.1	25	6.2	57.0	12.1	804	445	83	964
Utah	407	367.25	351	222	72	456	54.8	0	5.5	50.5	12.2	865	429	69	739
Ariz.	478	485.50	430	246	72	426	44.4	22	15.6	67.2	11.3	816	354	63	442

Table B–9 Comparison of Areal Units on Dependent Variable: Public School Expenditures Per Pupil, 1965

State	y_{126}	$\bar{y}$	x_{125}	x_{36}	x_{48}	x_{85}	x_{113}	x_{82}	x_{13}
					Variable				
Massachusetts	520	543.54	528	140	465	344	321	315	75.0
Connecticut	637	643.37	600	135	533	564	690	291	75.5
North Carolina	379	352.49	322	102	296	318	−1627	209	35.0
South Carolina	349	370.01	284	85	260	117	−2050	202	0
Oregon	612	627.51	569	138	518	380	966	298	96.7
Washington	556	556.02	534	138	495	540	964	347	97.0
Utah	459	487.01	407	123	351	269	739	310	96.8
Arizona	514	467.94	478	136	430	276	442	318	80.0

Table B-10 Comparison of Areal Units on Dependent Variable:
Per Capita Educational Expenditures of State and Local Governments, 1965

State	y_{127}	$\bar{y}$	x_{73}	x_{120}	x_{40}	x_{29}	x_{113}	x_{82}
					Variable			
Massachusetts	122	117.18	90	55	406	502	321	315
Connecticut	140	103.40	102	19	459	544	690	291
North Carolina	117	112.85	87	2	182	296	−1627	209
South Carolina	103	99.55	78	331	135	274	−2050	202
Oregon	204	192.00	145	15	293	448	966	341
Washington	189	201.60	148	209	352	445	964	347
Utah	219	216.21	162	27	306	429	739	310
Arizona	185	189.33	138	18	219	354	442	318

Table B–11   Comparison of Areal Units on Dependent Variable:
Per Capita Educational Expenditures of State and Local Governments, 1966

State	y_{128}	$\bar{y}$	x_{127}	x_{111}	x_{69}	x_{12}	x_{20}	x_{70}
				Variable				
Massachusetts	133	149.36	122	414	58	700	22	522
Connecticut	151	170.05	140	404	56	722	42	550
North Carolina	137	161.95	117	465	96	80	245	630
South Carolina	118	131.81	103	474	100	0	348	999
Oregon	223	243.39	204	411	54	600	10	542
Washington	207	213.99	189	413	65	694	17	528
Utah	256	239.02	219	394	55	959	5	553
Arizona	210	203.86	185	445	91	286	33	569

Table B-12 Comparison of Areal Units on Dependent Variable:
Percentage of School Revenues from State, 1964

State	y_{135}	$\bar{y}$	x_{16}	x_{51}	x_{85}	x_{120}	x_{12}	x_{111}	x_{96}	x_{99}	x_{69}	x_{124}
						Variable						
Massachusetts	25.1	31.86	625	96	344	5.5	700	414	57.5	13.6	58	7.7
Connecticut	36.3	46.97	377	81	564	1.9	722	404	56.0	16.5	56	8.6
North Carolina	74.7	84.25	825	61	369	.2	800	465	69.0	3.9	96	5.3
South Carolina	72.1	62.88	100	52	117	33.1	0	474	99.9	6.5	100	5.6
Oregon	33.9	32.02	517	71	380	1.5	600	411	80.0	26.3	54	6.8
Washington	64.9	69.06	515	83	540	20.9	694	413	65.3	45.6	65	6.6
Utah	53.8	54.88	468	69	269	2.7	959	394	44.7	17.2	55	7.2
Arizona	37.2	32.42	600	63	276	1.8	286	445	90.7	27.4	91	3.3

Table B-13 Comparison of Areal Units on Dependent Variable: Percentage of School Revenues from State, 1965

State	y_{136}	$\bar{y}$	x_{135}	x_{90}	x_{53}	x_{120}	x_{12}	x_{69}	x_{20}
					Variable				
Massachusetts	22.1	19.83	25.1	13.6	136	5.5	70.0	58	22
Connecticut	32.8	30.01	36.3	16.5	102	1.9	72.2	56	42
North Carolina	65.9	53.26	74.7	3.9	66	.2	8.0	96	245
South Carolina	59.7	55.79	72.1	6.5	63	33.1	0	100	348
Oregon	26.5	28.35	33.9	26.3	90	1.5	60.0	54	10
Washington	58.3	61.86	64.9	45.6	102	20.9	69.4	65	17
Utah	49.0	51.22	53.8	17.2	72	2.7	95.9	55	5
Arizona	36.3	36.91	37.2	27.4	72	1.8	28.6	91	33

233

Table B-14 Comparison of Areal Units on Dependent Variable:
Expenditures for Higher Education Per Capita, 1963

State	y_{55}	$\bar{y}$	x_{44}	x_{86}	x_{85}	x_{43}
			Variable			
Massachusetts	9.80	26.99	185	15	344	110
Connecticut	13.90	31.71	195	8	564	103
North Carolina	21.60	28.29	183	10	369	146
South Carolina	15.40	20.86	163	9	117	164
Oregon	45.10	35.41	257	12	380	194
Washington	43.50	40.21	285	16	540	149
Utah	54.50	34.01	251	11	269	238
Arizona	40.70	28.39	224	10	276	166

Table B-15 Comparison of Areal Units on Dependent Variable:
Expenditures for Higher Education Per Capita, 1964

State	y_{143}	$\bar{y}$	Variable x_{123}	x_{50}
Massachusetts	96.40	64.90	629	25.1
Connecticut	47.30	58.23	568	25.4
North Carolina	43.08	42.91	430	26.2
South Carolina	25.00	29.75	347	28.8
Oregon	53.15	58.43	544	24.0
Washington	51.10	53.34	510	24.9
Utah	71.00	39.39	447	29.0
Arizona	42.30	37.55	384	26.6

Table B-16 Comparison of Areal Units on Educational Variable: Expenditures for Higher Education Per Capita, 1966

State	y_{144}	$\bar{y}$	x_{143}	x_{119}	x_{43}	x_{72}	x_{85}	x_{39}
				Variable				
Massachusetts	121.20	113.55	96.40	2.4	110	48	344	40
Connecticut	67.30	55.82	47.30	33.4	103	29	564	37
North Carolina	56.40	50.81	43.08	2.3	146	58	369	35
South Carolina	35.20	29.46	25.00	0	164	82	117	37
Oregon	79.00	62.29	53.15	24.1	194	40	380	61
Washington	69.90	60.30	51.10	33.4	149	53	540	53
Utah	102.90	83.74	71.00	20.9	238	55	269	68
Arizona	56.00	49.89	42.30	47.8	166	77	276	60

Table B-17 Comparison of Areal Units on Dependent Variable:
Number of Students Per Classroom, 1964

State	y_{50}	Variable $\bar{y}$	x_{15}
Massachusetts	25.1	25.92	65.0
Connecticut	25.4	25.91	63.9
North Carolina	26.2	26.22	96.0
South Carolina	28.8	25.39	100.0
Oregon	24.0	25.30	70.0
Washington	24.9	25.92	65.4
Utah	29.0	25.75	48.0
Arizona	26.6	26.12	85.8

Table B–18 Comparison of Areal Units on Dependent Variable: Number of Students Per Classroom, 1965

State	y_{145}	Variable $\bar{y}$	x_{50}
Massachusetts	26.5	24.89	25.1
Connecticut	24.8	25.15	25.4
North Carolina	25.3	25.86	26.2
South Carolina	28.4	28.14	28.8
Oregon	23.7	23.92	24.0
Washington	27.3	24.71	24.9
Utah	28.3	28.32	29.0
Arizona	26.8	26.21	26.6

Table B-19 Comparison of Areal Units on Dependent Variable: Number of Students Per Classroom, 1966

State	y_{146}	$\bar{y}$	x_{145}	Variable x_8	x_{85}	x_{10}	x_{15}
Massachusetts	27.7	25.53	26.5	198	344	88	65.0
Connecticut	20.8	23.91	24.8	75	564	48	63.9
North Carolina	24.7	24.38	25.3	76	369	15	96.0
South Carolina	27.3	27.36	28.4	79	117	32	100.0
Oregon	24.4	22.84	23.7	122	380	40	70.0
Washington	25.0	26.31	27.3	77	540	24	65.4
Utah	27.8	27.27	28.3	52	269	16	48.0
Arizona	25.0	25.82	26.8	131	276	37	85.8

Index

240

Date Due